I0211168

JAMES

THE TEACHER'S OUTLINE & STUDY BIBLE™

NEW TESTAMENT

KING JAMES VERSION

Leadership Ministries Worldwide
Chattanooga, TN

DEDICATED

To all the men and women of the world who preach and teach the Gospel of our Lord Jesus Christ and to the Mercy and Grace of God

&

- Demonstrated to us in Christ Jesus our Lord.

    "In whom we have redemption through His blood, the forgiveness of sins, according to the riches of His grace." (Ep.1:7)

- Out of the mercy and grace of God, His Word has flowed. Let every person know that God will have mercy upon him, forgiving and using him to fulfill His glorious plan of salvation.

    "For God so loved the world, that he gave His only begotten Son, that whosoever believeth in Him should not perish, but have everlasting life. For God sent not his son into the world to condemn the world, but that the world through him might be saved." (Jn.3:16-17)

    "For this is good and acceptable in the sight of God our Saviour; who will have all men to be saved, and to come unto the knowledge of the truth." (1 Ti.2:3-4)

The Teacher's Outline & Study Bible™

is written for God's servants to use in their study, teaching, and preaching of God's Holy Word...

- to share the Word of God with the world.
- to help believers, both ministers and laypersons, in their understanding, preaching, and teaching of God's Word.
- to do everything we possibly can to lead men, women, boys, and girls to give their hearts and lives to Jesus Christ and to secure the eternal life that He offers.
- to do all we can to minister to the needy of the world.
- to give Jesus Christ His proper place, the place the Word gives Him. Therefore, no work of Leadership Ministries Worldwide—no Outline Bible Resources—will ever be personalized.

6/13

How To Use

THE TEACHER'S OUTLINE AND STUDY BIBLE™
(TOSB)

To gain maximum benefit, here is all you do. Follow these easy steps, using the sample outline below.

1 STUDY TITLE

2 MAJOR POINTS

3 SUBPOINTS

**4 COMMENTARY,
QUESTIONS,
APPLICATION,
ILLUSTRATIONS**
(Follows Scripture)

1. First: Read the **Study Title** two or three times so that the subject sinks in.

2. Then: Read the **Study Title** and the **Major Points** (Pts.1,2,3) together quickly. Do this several times and you will quickly grasp the overall theme of the Scripture.

B. The Steps to Peace (Part II): Prayer & Positive Thinking, 4:6-9

1. Peace comes through prayer
 a. The charge: Do not worry or be anxious
 b. The remedy: Prayer
  1) About everything
  2) With requests
  3) With thanksgiving
 c. The promise: Peace
  1) Peace that passes all understanding
  2) Peace that keeps our hearts & minds
2. Peace comes through positive thinking
 a. The charge: Think & practice things that are...
  1) True
  2) Honest
  3) Just
  4) Pure

6 Be careful for nothing; but in every thing by prayer and supplication with thanksgiving let your requests be made known unto God.
7 And the peace of God, which passeth all understanding, shall keep your hearts and minds through Christ Jesus.
8 Finally, brethren, whatsoever things are true, whatsoever things are honest, whatsoever things are just, whatsoever things are pure, whatsoever things are lovely, whatsoever

---

3. Now: Read both the **Major Points** and **Subpoints**. Note how the points are beside the applicable verse and simply state what the Scripture is saying—in *Outline* form.

4. Read the **Commentary**. As you read and re-read, pray that the Holy Spirit will bring to your attention exactly what you should study and teach. It's all there, outlined and fully developed, just waiting for you to explore!

TEACHERS, PLEASE NOTE:

⇒ Cover the **Scripture** and the **Major Points** with your students. Drive the **Scripture** and **Major Points** into their hearts and minds.

(Continue on next page)

⇒ Cover *only some of the commentary* with your students, not all (unless, of course, you have plenty of time). Cover only as much commentary as is needed to get across the major points.

Do NOT feel that you must...
- cover all the commentary under each point
- share every illustration
- ask all the questions

An abundance of commentary is given so you can find just what you need for...
- your own style of teaching
- your own emphasis
- your own class needs

PLEASE NOTE: It is of utmost importance that you (and your study group) grasp the Scripture, the Study Title, and the Major Points. It is this that the Holy Spirit will make alive to your heart and that you will more likely remember and use day by day.

MAJOR POINTS include:

APPLICATIONS:
Use these to show how the Scripture applies to everyday life.

ILLUSTRATIONS:
Simply a window that allows enough light in the lesson so a point can be more clearly seen. A suggestion: Do not just "read" through an illustration if the illustration is a story, but learn it and make it your own. Then give the illustration life by communicating it with *excitement & energy*.

QUESTIONS:
These are designed to stimulate thought and discussion.

A CLOSER LOOK:
In some of the studies, you will see a portion boxed in and entitled: "A Closer Look." This discussion will be a closer study on a particular point. It is generally too detailed for a Sunday School class session, but more adaptable for personal study or an in-depth Bible Study class.

PERSONAL JOURNAL:
At the close of every lesson there is space for you to record brief thoughts regarding the impact of the lesson on your life. As you study through the Bible, you will find these comments invaluable as you look back upon them.

Now, may our wonderful Lord bless you mightily as you study and teach His Holy Word. And may our Lord grant you much fruit: many who will become greater servants and witnesses for Him.

ABBREVIATIONS

&	= and		O.T.	= Old Testament
bc.	= because		p./pp.	= page/pages
concl.	= conclusion		pt.	= point
cp.	= compare		quest.	= question
ct.	= contrast		rel.	= religion
e.g.	= for example		rgt.	= righteousness
f.	= following		thru	= through
illust.	= illustration		v./vv.	= verse/verses
k.	= Kingdom, K. of God, K. of Heaven		vs.	= versus

THE BOOKS OF THE OLD TESTAMENT

Book	Abbreviation	Book	Abbreviation
Genesis	Gen. or Ge.	Ecclesiastes	Eccl. or Ec.
Exodus	Ex.	The Song of Solomon	S. of Sol. or Song
Leviticus	Lev. or Le.		
Numbers	Num. or Nu.	Isaiah	Is.
Deuteronomy	Dt. or De.	Jeremiah	Jer. or Je.
Joshua	Josh. or Jos.	Lamentations	Lam.
Judges	Judg. or Jud.	Ezekiel	Ezk. or Eze.
Ruth	Ruth or Ru.	Daniel	Dan. or Da.
1 Samuel	1 Sam. or 1 S.	Hosea	Hos. or Ho.
2 Samuel	2 Sam. or 2 S.	Joel	Joel
1 Kings	1 Ki. or 1 K.	Amos	Amos or Am.
2 Kings	2 Ki. or 2 K.	Obadiah	Obad. or Ob.
1 Chronicles	1 Chron. or 1 Chr.	Jonah	Jon. or Jona.
2 Chronicles	2 Chron. or 2 Chr.	Micah	Mic. or Mi.
Ezra	Ezra or Ezr.	Nahum	Nah. or Na.
Nehemiah	Neh. or Ne.	Habakkuk	Hab.
Esther	Est.	Zephaniah	Zeph. or Zep.
Job	Job or Jb.	Haggai	Hag.
Psalms	Ps.	Zechariah	Zech. or Zec.
Proverbs	Pr.	Malachi	Mal.

THE BOOKS OF THE NEW TESTAMENT

Book	Abbreviation	Book	Abbreviation
Matthew	Mt.	1 Timothy	1 Tim. or 1 Ti.
Mark	Mk.	2 Timothy	2 Tim. or 2 Ti.
Luke	Lk. or Lu.	Titus	Tit.
John	Jn.	Philemon	Phile. or Phm.
The Acts	Acts or Ac.	Hebrews	Heb. or He.
Romans	Ro.	James	Jas. or Js.
1 Corinthians	1 Cor. or 1 Co.	1 Peter	1 Pt. or 1 Pe.
2 Corinthians	2 Cor. or 2 Co.	2 Peter	2 Pt. or 2 Pe.
Galatians	Gal. or Ga.	1 John	1 Jn.
Ephesians	Eph. or Ep.	2 John	2 Jn.
Philippians	Ph.	3 John	3 Jn.
Colossians	Col.	Jude	Jude
1 Thessalonians	1 Th.	Revelation	Rev. or Re.
2 Thessalonians	2 Th.		

*"Go ye therefore, and
teach all nations"*
(Mt.28:19)

TABLE OF CONTENTS

JAMES

THE TEACHER'S OUTLINE & STUDY BIBLE™ is *unique*. It differs from all other Study Bibles and Teaching Materials in that every Passage and Subject is outlined right beside the Scripture. When you choose any *Subject* below and turn to the reference, you have not only the Scripture but also the Subject *already outlined for you—verse by verse.*

For a quick example, choose one of the subjects below and turn over to the Scripture—you will find this to be a marvelous help for faster, easier, and more meaningful study of Scripture. *In addition, every point* of the Scripture and Subject is *fully developed in a Commentary with* these Unique Features: Personal Application, Illustrations, Questions, and much more! Again, this arrangement makes study preparation much easier and faster.

A suggestion: For the quickest overview of *1 Thessalonians*, first read *all the major titles* (I, II, III, etc.), then come back and read the subtitles.

JAMES

	Page
HOW TO USE	i
ABBREVIATIONS	iii
INTRODUCTION TO JAMES	1
GREETING: THE SERVANT OF GOD ADDRESSES BELIEVERS WORLDWIDE, 1:1	5

I. TEMPTATIONS AND TRIALS: THE BASIC FACTS, 1:2-27
A. The Essential Attitude to Trials and Temptation: Joy, 1:2-4	10
B. The Way To Conquer Trials and Temptation, 1:5-12	15
C. The Origin of Trials and Temptation, 1:13-18	22
D. The Preparations Necessary to Withstand Trials and Temptation, 1:19-27	28

II. TEMPTATIONS AND TRIALS: COMMON TO ALL CHRISTIAN BELIEVERS, 2:1-26
A. Temptation 1: Showing Partiality and Favoritism, 2:1-13	34
B. Temptation 2: Professing Faith Without Works, 2:14-26	42

III. TEMPTATIONS AND TRIALS: COMMON TO ALL, BUT ESPECIALLY TO TEACHERS, 3:1-18
A. Temptation 1: Misusing the Tongue, 3:1-12	49
B. Temptation 2: Misunderstanding and Twisting True Wisdom, 3:13-18	56

Page

IV. TEMPTATIONS AND TRIALS: TRIUMPHANTLY OVERCOME,
4:1-10

    A. The causes of Temptation and Wrongdoing, 4:1-6   65
    B. The Way to Overcome Temptation, 4:7-10   75

V, TEMPTATIONS AND TRIALS: COMMON TO ALL BUT
ESPECIALLY TO THE GIFTED, 4:11-5:6

    A. Temptation 1: The Judge—Judging Others, 4:11-12   82
    B. Temptation 2: The Humanist—Boasting Self-Sufficiency,
       4:13-17   88
    C. Temptation 3: The Rich Man—Hoarding Wealth, 5:1-6   94

VI. TEMPTATIONS AND TRIALS: COMBATED STEP BY STEP, 5:7-20

    A. Step 1: Be Patient—Endure—Keep Your Eyes Focused
       Upon the Return of the Lord, 5:7-11   101
    B. Step 2: Take Each Circumstance and Respond Properly,
       5:12-20   107

OUTLINE & SUBJECT INDEX   125

ILLUSTRATION INDEX   133

ACKNOWLEDGMENTS   141

THE GENERAL EPISTLE OF

JAMES

INTRODUCTION

AUTHOR: Uncertain. Probably James the Lord's brother. Note these facts.

1. There are three other men named James who are mentioned in the New Testament.

⇒ There was the Apostle James, who was the Son of Zebedee and the brother of the Apostle John. It is almost impossible that he could have been the author, for he was martyred by Herod Agrippa about A.D. 44. This was some years before the letter of James was written.

⇒ There was the Apostle James the less, who was the son of Alpheus and who was also the cousin of Jesus. He is a possibility, but so little is known about him that it is highly unlikely that he is the author.

⇒ There was James, the father of the Apostle Judas (Lu.6:16, NASB). Nothing else is know about this James.

2. James, the Lord's brother, was well known by all believers everywhere. Being the Lord's brother was enough to give him a world-wide reputation among believers. In addition to this, he was the pastor of the great Jerusalem church which was the mother church of Christianity. Note in verse one that he simply calls himself James. He needed no other identification; everyone knew the James who was writing the letter. The point is this:

⇒ James the Lord's brother was so well known that any other James would have had to identify himself to keep from being mistaken as James the Lord's brother.

3. Some argue that if the author was really James the Lord's brother, he would have mentioned the fact. A.T. Robertson has an excellent answer to this position:

> *If it be urged that the author of the epistle, if related to Jesus, would have said so, one may reply that a delicate sense of propriety may have had precisely the opposite effect. Jesus had himself laid emphasis on the fact of his spiritual kinship with all believers as more important (Matt.12:48-50). The fact that James during the ministry of Jesus was not sympathetic with His work would also act as a restraining force upon him. The brother of Jesus (see also Jude 1) naturally would wish to make his appeal on the same plane as the other teachers of the gospel. He rejoices in the title of 'servant of God and of the Lord Jesus Christ,' just as Paul did later (Rom.1:1; Phil.1:1; Titus 1:1) and as Jude, the brother of James, did (Jude 1).[1]*

4. The church, from the very earliest of its tradition, has held that the author was James the Lord's brother. As RVG Tasker says,

> *The tradition that became established in the Church that the Epistle was not only apostolic but should be attributed to James, the head of the Early Church at*

---

[1] A.T. Robertson. *Studies in the Epistle of James.* (Nashville, TN: Broadman Press, 1930), p.2.

Jerusalem, ought undoubtedly to be accepted as true. Not only is it incapable of being scientifically disproved, but it has much intrinsic probability. [2]

5. The facts about James the Lord's brother point toward him being the author.
   ⇒ He was a brother of the Lord (Mt.13:55; Mk.6:3).
   ⇒ He was an eyewitness of the risen Lord. In fact, the Lord appeared to him in a private conversation (1 Co.15:7). He was among those waiting for the coming of the Spirit in the Upper Room (Ac.1:14).
   ⇒ He was an apostle. He was probably appointed after his private encounter with the risen Lord (Ga.1:19).
   ⇒ He became the pastor of the great Jerusalem Church. He probably assumed his duties when Peter left on his missionary journeys (Ac.12:17; etc.). Thereafter, he is by far the greatest personality in the Jerusalem Church.
   ⇒ He was the first one told about Peter's release from prison (Ac.12:17).
   ⇒ He was the presiding officer over the great Jerusalem Council (Ac.15).
   ⇒ He was called a pillar of the church along with Peter and John. Paul was forced to discuss his ministry among the Gentiles with him as well as with Peter and John (Ga.1:19; 2:9).
   ⇒ He was the one who received the offerings brought by Paul from the Gentile churches to help the Jerusalem saints (Ac.21:18-25).
   ⇒ He was well versed in the Old Testament (see Ac.15:15f; *book of James*).
   ⇒ He was familiar with Jesus' teachings. The epistle has around twenty quotations from the Sermon on the Mount alone.

DATE: Uncertain. Probably A.D. 45-50.

The date is disputed. Some say it is one of the earliest writings, perhaps the earliest. Others say it is a later writing. However, the arguments for the earlier date seem to fit the book more readily.

1. The church is still described in its primitive form. The word "assembly" (Greek, *synagogue*) is used instead of *church* (Js.2:2), and the elders of the church are mentioned, but the deacons and bishops are not (Js.5:14).

2. There is no mention of the Jewish-Gentile controversy nor of the great church council held in Jerusalem in A.D. 50 (Ac.15).

3. The book is a picture of what primitive Christianity meant to a Jew converted to Christ. It leaves one with the sense of *birth-pangs*, of a great transition occurring from a Jewish to a Christian way of life.

TO WHOM WRITTEN: "To the twelve tribes which are scattered abroad." It was written to Christians of the dispersion (diaspora). The word dispersion simply means to the Jews scattered around the world.

PURPOSE: James had two purposes for writing.

1. To correct a corrupted faith that was rapidly seeping into the church. Many were professing faith in Christ, but living immoral and unrighteous lives. Their faith was profession only—a faith of license with little or no restraint upon behavior.

2. To present the true faith of Christ: a faith of the heart—a faith that produces outward fruit. James's point is very simple: a person is known to be a Christian only by his behavior. What he does proves one of two things: it proves he is a Christian or it proves he is not a Christian.

---

2 RVG Tasker. *The General Epistle of James.* "Tyndale New Testament Commentaries." (Grand Rapids, MI: Eerdmans Publishing Co., 1956), p.21.

INTRODUCTION

SPECIAL FEATURES:

1. James is "A General or Catholic Epistle." That is, it is not written to a specific church or individual, but rather, it is written to all Christian believers. James is written particularly to all Jewish converts.

2. James is "The Epistle of the Royal Law." That is, it is the epistle stressing the necessity for loving one's neighbor as oneself. The law of Moses is called the law of liberty (Js.2:8-12).

3. James is "The Epistle of Sermon Notes." The characteristics of the Jewish and Greek sermons of that day are found throughout James. The epistle seems to be a collection of sermon notes centered around the theme of trials and temptations.

4. James is "The Epistle of Practical Living" or "The Epistle of the Second Stage." Its concern is the life of the believer after he has become a Christian and has been assured of his salvation. The thrust is Christian growth.

THE GENERAL EPISTLE OF

JAMES

<table>
<tr><td></td><td>CHAPTER 1

GREETING:
THE SERVANT OF
GOD ADDRESSES
BELIEVERS
WORLDWIDE, 1:1</td></tr>
<tr><td>1. The servant of God, James
2. The believers scattered all over the world</td><td>James, a servant of God and of the Lord Jesus Christ, to the twelve tribes which are scattered abroad, greeting.</td></tr>
</table>

GREETING: THE SERVANT OF GOD ADDRESSES BELIEVERS WORLDWIDE
James 1:1

INTRODUCTORY STUDY: THE SERVANT OF GOD WRITES TO BELIEVERS EVERYWHERE

Text: **James 1:1**

Aim: To live and be known as a servant of Christ.

Memory Verse:

> **"James, a servant of God and of the Lord Jesus Christ, to the twelve tribes which are scattered abroad, greeting" (James 1:1).**

INTRODUCTION:
Apart from your job, your hobbies, and your achievements, think about this question: What are you known for—you personally? The answer to this question will likely reveal whether you are motivated toward spiritual things. Do people think of you as someone who regularly attends church? Is it common to find you:
- ⇒ working in the local church?
- ⇒ witnessing to others?
- ⇒ helping others in various ways?
- ⇒ reaching out and ministering to those in need?

The introduction to the book of *James* is a most interesting passage of Scripture. It tells us some facts about one of the brothers of the Lord Jesus, facts about a person who lived with Jesus day by day and had the opportunity to notice what kind of life He lived. The passage is also a dynamic challenge to us. The powerful example of love and evangelism left by the Apostle James leads us to an inescapable and urgent question: What would happen if we gave our hearts to world missions and to reach the lost with the same degree of love that James did? Note two points in verse one:

OUTLINE:
1. The servant of God, James (v.1).
2. The believers scattered all over the world (v.1).

1. THE SERVANT OF GOD, JAMES (v.1).

James was apparently so well-known among the believers throughout the world that no title was needed other than his name. This points rather strongly toward his being James, the Lord's brother. Note two touching and very important facts about what James says.

1. He simply calls himself James, "a servant of God and of the Lord Jesus Christ." He is a world renowned leader among God's people. Yet his glory is not in the title of his position, but in the fact that he is a servant of God and of Christ. Despite his position and worldwide reputation, what matters to him most is the intimacy of his relationship to God and his Lord. This is clearly seen when the word *servant* is understood, for the meaning of the word shows that James deliberately chose the word to describe his relationship to the Lord.

The word "servant" here means far more than just serving a person or group of people. It means to be a slave totally possessed by the master. It means to be a *bondservant* bound by law to a master. A look at the slave-market of James's day shows more clearly what James meant when he said he was a "slave of Jesus Christ."

   a. The slave was owned and totally possessed by his master. James was purchased and possessed by Christ, the Son of the living God. Christ had looked upon him and had seen his rebellious and needful condition. And when Christ looked, the most wonderful thing happened: Christ loved him and bought him; therefore, he was now the possession of Christ.
   b. The slave existed for his master and he had no other reason for existence. He had no personal rights whatsoever. James's rights were the rights of Christ only.
   c. The slave served his master and he existed only for the purpose of service. James lived only to serve Christ—hour by hour and day by day.
   d. The slave's will belonged to his master. He was allowed no will and no ambition other than the will and ambition of the master. James was completely obedient to the will of the master. James belonged to Christ.
   e. There is a fifth and most precious thing that James meant by "a slave of Jesus Christ." He meant that he had the highest and most honored and kingly profession in all the world. Men of God, the greatest men of history, have always been called "the servants of God." It is the highest title of honor. The believer's slavery to Jesus Christ is no cringing, cowardly, shameful subjection. It is the position of honor—the honor that bestows upon a man the privileges and responsibilities of serving the King of kings and Lord of lords.

> **"If any man serve me, let him follow me; and where I am, there shall also my servant be: if any man serve me, him will my Father honour" (Jn.12:26; see Ro.12:1; 1 Co.15:58).**
>
> **"Serve the Lord with gladness: come before his presence with singing" (Ps.100:2).**

ILLUSTRATION:

> *The great violinist, Nicolo Paganini, willed his marvelous violin to Genoa—the city of his birth—but only on condition that the instrument never be played. It was an unfortunate condition, for it is a peculiarity of wood that as long as it is used and handled, it shows little wear. As soon as it is discarded, it begins to decay.*
>
> *The exquisite mellow-toned violin now has become worm-eaten in its beautiful case, valueless except as a relic. The moldering instrument is a reminder that a life withdrawn from service to others loses its meaning.*

James's strong emphasis upon service is illustrated well! In order to retain our value and our worth and not degenerate into a worthless relic, we should serve and remain active. "But whosoever will be great among you, let him be your minister. And whosoever will be chief among you, let him be your servant (Matt.20:26, 27)."[3]

2. James says that Jesus, the carpenter from Nazareth, was the Lord Jesus Christ.
   ⇒ By "Lord" he meant God. The word Lord is frequently used in the Old Testament Scripture to mean God.[4]
   ⇒ By "Christ" he meant the Messiah, the anointed Savior whom God had promised down through the centuries.

Just imagine the daily, monthly, and yearly contact James had with Jesus, and still James calls Him...
   • the Lord Jesus Christ, the Lord and Christ of the Old Testament Scriptures
   • the Lord of glory (Js.2:1)
   • the Lord who is coming again (Js.5:7)
   • the Lord whose coming draws near (Js.5:8)

The point is this: James is saying that the Lord Jesus Christ is God, the very Son of God who is equal to God the Father. He is saying that his brother, Jesus the carpenter from Nazareth, is of the very nature and character of God, of the very being and essence of God.

> **"Therefore let all the house of Israel know assuredly, that God hath made that same Jesus, whom ye have crucified, both Lord and Christ" (Ac.2:36).**

QUESTIONS:
1. What does it mean to be a "servant" of Jesus Christ? Are you one?
2. In what ways has God called you to be a servant of Jesus Christ?

2. THE BELIEVERS SCATTERED ALL OVER THE WORLD (v.1).

The believers James was writing to were everywhere, in all parts of the known world. But note two significant points.

1. First, James is writing to a specific group of believers: the believers of the twelve tribes of Israel. How could this be when the twelve tribes had been scattered all over the world and had lost their identity?

This very fact gives us the answer. James is not writing to *each of the tribes* of Israel; he is writing to *all the tribes* of Israel—to all Jews wherever they might be. He is referring to all Israel, not wanting a single Jew to feel left out of his message. As the brother of the Lord Jesus Christ and as the pastor of the great Jerusalem church, what he had to say was imperative for all to hear and heed.

2. Second, James loved his people with an unusual love. They were deeply rooted in his heart, and he felt a strong calling to reach out and exhort them in the Lord. This is the very reason he was writing to them. Just think—his letter could be passed from church to church and from synagogue to synagogue all over the world. James either laid out the plans and followed through in seeing that the plans were carried out or else the Holy Spirit gave him assurance that his letter would be spread to all the Jews scat-

---

3 Ted Kyle and John Todd. *A Treasury of Bible Illustrations.* (Chattanooga, TN: AMG Publishers, 1995), #150.
4 A.T. Robertson. *Word Pictures in the New Testament*, Vol.6. (Nashville, TN: Broadman Press, 1933), p.10.

tered across the world. James had some indication that he would be reaching all Jews, and his heart longed to reach the millions from the twelve tribes scattered all over the earth.

The point to see is the love and the evangelistic heart James had for his people. True, he was writing primarily to Jewish believers, but he was also doing what he said: sending greetings to the twelve tribes scattered abroad. What he says is applicable to all believers of all generations.

APPLICATION:

What a dynamic example for us of love and true evangelism. What would happen if our own hearts beat with the same degree of love and evangelism—the compassion to reach the lost and suffering people of our communities, cities, and nations? Look at the worldwide compassion of James. He was making an attempt to reach his people all over the world. Where is the heart for missions today? Where is the person who will totally give his or her heart to world missions and evangelism?

> **"But ye shall receive power, after that the Holy Ghost is come upon you: and ye shall be witnesses unto me both in Jerusalem, and in all Judaea, and in Samaria, and unto the uttermost part of the earth" (Ac.1:8).**

ILLUSTRATION:

The Apostle James was one of the first martyrs, paying the ultimate price for being a follower of Christ. People like that do not just *talk* about being servants; they *show* that they are servants—they live it.

> *[Some years after James was martyred] a brilliant man named Tertullian said that it was not arguments that converted him to Christianity, because he could counter any point. [Tertullian's revealing testimony was:] "But they demonstrated something I didn't have. The thing that converted me to Christianity was the way they loved each other."*[5]

QUESTIONS:

1. Even though James wrote to first century Jewish Christians, how does his message apply to believers of all times?
2. How can you follow James's example of love and evangelism?

SUMMARY:

A person may have many duties and obligations, but for believers, one is first in importance, of the very highest priority. As believers, we have the duty to live out the gospel, that is, to tell about it with both our words and our lives. We must bear testimony that Jesus has made a way for every person to be a part of His family. The Apostle James is a shining example of the kind of servant we all need to be. We must, as James did, identify ourselves as...

1. Servants of God.
2. Believers among all believers worldwide.

---

[5] G. Curtis Jones. *1000 Illustrations for Preaching and Teaching.* (Nashville, TN: Broadman Press, 1986), p.220.

JAMES 1:1

PERSONAL JOURNAL NOTES:
(Reflection and Response)

1. The most important thing that I learned from this lesson was:

2. The thing that I need to work on the most is:

3. I can apply this lesson to my life by:

4. Closing Prayer of Commitment:

	I. TEMPTATIONS & TRIALS: THE BASIC FACTS, 1:2-27
	A. The Essential Attitude Toward Trials & Temptation: Joy, 1:2-4
1. The fact: Will have trials & temptations	2 My brethren, count it all joy when ye fall into divers temptations;
2. The needed attitude: Joy	
a. Achieved by knowing that trials & temptations develop patience	3 Knowing this, that the trying of your faith worketh patience.
b. Achieved by persevering	4 But let patience have her perfect work, that ye may be perfect and entire, wanting nothing.
3. The result: Makes us mature & complete	

Section I
TEMPTATIONS AND TRIALS: THE BASIC FACTS
James 1:2-27

STUDY 1: THE ESSENTIAL ATTITUDE TOWARD TRIALS AND TEMPTATION: JOY

Text: James 1:2-4

Aim: To work at being joyful during trials and temptations.

Memory Verse:

> **"Knowing this, that the trying of your faith worketh patience" (James 1:3).**

INTRODUCTION:
The path of life is not an easy path to walk. It is filled with all kinds of trials and temptations, trials such as sickness, disease, accidents, disappointments, suffering, and death, and endless temptations that seduce us into sin and evil. What we need is a guaranteed way to conquer all the trials and temptations of life. This is the glorious message of this passage: there is a way to conquer and triumph in this life, no matter how severe the trial or temptation. What is the way? It is possessing and experiencing a true spirit of joy and perseverance as we face the trials and temptations of life. This is a striking study on enduring faith. Faith, real faith that comes from God above, endures all trials. It will not fail. Such faith is complete, full, perfected.

OUTLINE:
1. The fact: we will have trials and temptations (v.2).
2. The needed attitude: joy (vv.2-4).
3. The result: makes us perfect and entire (v.4).

1. THE FACT: WILL HAVE TRIALS AND TEMPTATIONS (v.2).

We all go through many common temptations and trials in life. Life is often hard. But note that the word James uses for temptations or trials throughout the book of James means far more than just to tempt; it means...

> to test
> to try
> to prove

That is, the temptations and trials of life are there to prove us; they are for a beneficial purpose; they are permitted by God for a good purpose.[6] What is that purpose? To make us stronger and purer.

⇒ When we conquer temptation, we become a much more pure person—more holy, righteous, and just.

⇒ When we triumphantly go through the trials of life, we become a much stronger person—more steadfast, enduring, and persevering

⇒ When we stand up against trials and temptations, we become a dynamic witness to all those who see us: we demonstrate the living presence and power of Christ—that He actually does live in our hearts and lives and is going to give us eternal life.

Note one other thing that James says: he says that we will *fall into all kinds* of temptations and trials. The Greek scholar A.T. Robertson says, "It is the picture of being *surrounded...by trials.*"[7] But we must always remember: no matter what the trial or temptation, it is for our good and for our benefit. It is to help us. It is to prove us—to make us stronger and much more pure and righteous—to make us much more dynamic witnesses for Christ. God allows trials and temptations to make us more and more like Jesus.

"Now no chastening [trial] for the present seemeth to be joyous, but grievous: nevertheless afterward it yieldeth the peaceable fruit of righteousness unto them which are exercised thereby" (He.12:11).

ILLUSTRATION:

Even Abraham, Moses, Esther, and other great men and women of faith were tested. Testing and trials are not only useful, they are absolutely necessary. Each of us, every single Christian, will go through trials to test our faith.

> *Surrounded by scores of rough men in his army barracks, a young man considered simply going to bed his first night there, rather than his usual habit of kneeling by his bed to pray and read the Bible. In the face of temptation to hide his habit, he told himself, "I am a Christian. I will do just as I did at home!" The room was silent for a moment as the young man had his devotions, but no comment was made. The next night, however, eight others decided that they had to take action—they too got their Bibles and read and prayed. The new private became a shining example of Jesus Christ to every man in the company and won many souls for God.*

QUESTIONS:
1. How have you become more patient because of trials?
2. How have trials caused you to be more mature in Christ?
3. God wants us to be like His Son, Jesus. Name several ways we can become like Christ through our trials.

---

6 W.E. Vine. *Expository Dictionary of New Testament Words.* (Old Tappan, NJ: Fleming H. Revell Co., n.d.), p.116.
7 A.T. Robertson. *Word Pictures in the New Testament*, Vol.6, p.11.

2. THE NEEDED ATTITUDE: JOY (vv.2-4).

The attitude needed to face trials and temptations is joy. How is it even possible to have a spirit of joy at these times? How can a believer be joyful...

> when facing such trials as disease, accidents, disappointments, suffering, pain, and death?
>
> when facing enticing temptations?

Joy is usually not what fills our hearts when we face these things. When severe trials come our way, too often we despair and become discouraged and defeated. Most of us certainly do not rejoice.

There is only one way to face trials and temptations with a spirit of joy: we have to *switch our thinking,* turn our attitudes about trials and temptations completely around. We have to quit thinking negatively and think positively. In the words of Scripture, we must know something and we must do something.

1. We must know something: know that trials and temptations work patience (v.3). We must know this vital and valuable truth: trials and temptations are not to defeat and discourage us, but to prove us, to make us much stronger and more pure and righteous. The believer is to know that the trials and temptations of life will make him more steadfast, more persevering, and more enduring. They will make him much stronger, not weaker. They will make him more like Jesus. When the believer holds to this dynamic teaching without wavering, he can face trials and temptations much more positively. He can then begin to move toward the spirit of living joyfully in the face of trials and temptations.

2. We must do something: we must let patience work within us. As stated above, patience means to be steadfast, to persevere, and to endure. But it means far more than just bearing and putting up with the trials and temptations. It means far more than just following the advice of medicine and psychology: to take it easy; to be calm; to relax in stressful situations. Patience means...

> to persevere and keep on persevering, never giving in
>
> to take the initiative and to exert the energy and effort to conquer and to gain the victory over the trial and temptation

Now note the point: How can we joy or rejoice when a trial or temptation confronts us? By knowing that it will make us stronger, and then by persevering against it and conquering it. By knowing that it is an opportunity to make us more pure and more righteous like Jesus.

When we look at trials and temptations as opportunities, then we will begin to face them with joy. And when we begin to persevere and conquer them, then we will begin to walk through them in the joy of the Lord.

> **"Blessed is the man that endureth temptation: for when he is tried, he shall receive the crown of life, which the Lord hath promised to them that love him" (Js.1:12).**

ILLUSTRATION:

> *A young man staked out some land and began to dig for gold. Nearly two years later, most of his money and all of his patience were gone. Disgusted, he let the claim go.*
>
> *One week later, another man, taking advice from an old miner, staked his claim in the same spot. Within two days, he discovered one of the largest deposits of gold ever found. It didn't take long for news of the great find to spread through nearby towns. Other miners were quick to ask about the secret*

of the young miner's success. His humble reply was, "When the old miner advised me to take the claim, I decided right then and there I was going to see it through to the end no matter what. One thing I've learned about the success of the old miner—whether times are good or bad, he just keeps on digging."

The reward for perseverance is not always physical or tangible, but it is always worthwhile.

QUESTIONS:
1. How can you switch your thinking to have joy during trials?
2. Why do we need trials to make us stronger?
3. What one thing can you do to be truly victorious over trials and temptations?

3. THE RESULT: MAKES US MATURE AND COMPLETE (v.4).

The results of facing trials and temptations can be wonderful. When a person perseveres and conquers the trials and temptations of life, he or she becomes more perfect, more complete, more useful for a good and holy purpose. This does not mean "perfect" in the sense of becoming a perfect person, but having *perfection of purpose*. It has to do with an end, an aim, a goal, a purpose. It means fit, mature, fully grown at a particular stage of growth. For example, a fully grown child is a perfect child; he has reached his childhood and achieved the purpose of childhood. "Perfect" does not mean perfection of character, that is, being without sin. It is fitness, maturity for task and purpose. It is full development, maturity of godliness.

Being mature or grown up in Christ means at least two things.
1. First, when a person stands against trials and temptations and conquers them…
   he perfects the purpose God intended for him. That is, he becomes a stronger and more pure person—a person who is a little more like Jesus.
   he perfects his task and purpose for being on earth a little bit more

God has a twofold purpose for every believer: to become more and more like Jesus, and to do a specific task or job while on earth. When the believer perseveres against and conquers trials or temptations, he perfects both purposes a little bit more.
2. Second, a person becomes more and more complete in all parts.[8] This means a most wonderful thing. When a person perseveres and conquers trials or temptations…
   he becomes more entire, more fit, more sound, and more complete
   he also eliminates more weaknesses, more flaws, more defects, and more shortcomings

Day by day—trial by trial and temptation by temptation—he becomes stronger and more pure and righteous—more and more like the Lord Jesus. As the last two words of verse four say, "wanting nothing." The believer who faces trials and temptations in the joy of Christ conquers all, and he lacks nothing.

Such a person has all the abundance and fullness of life. He walks through life conquering and triumphing over all the trials and temptations of life, no matter how severe and stressful. It may even be death, but he stands fast in his faith and conquers death. And God rewards him with an eternity of perfection, fitness, completion, and fulfillment—all forever and ever. The believer is changed to permanently reflect the perfection of Jesus Christ.

---

8   A.T. Robertson. *Word Pictures in the New Testament*, Vol.6, p.12.

"Therefore leaving the principles of the doctrine of Christ, let us go on unto perfection; not laying again the foundation of repentance from dead works, and of faith toward God" (He.6:1).

ILLUSTRATION:
"Wisdom is the principal thing; therefore get wisdom: and with all thy getting get understanding" (Pr.4:7). Wisdom, maturity, becoming more and more like Christ—these are traits we all need. But we will not get them without trials.

Someone once observed, "It doesn't matter how much money you have, everyone has to buy wisdom on the installment plan."[9]

QUESTIONS:
1. Have you become wiser through your trials? In what way can you help others in their time of need or temptation?
2. You will never lack the necessities when you follow God's plan. Describe a particularly trying time in your life when God was faithful.

SUMMARY:

Trials and temptations can hang like dark clouds over our lives. But even when our souls are in torment, the Lord is faithfully working to make us complete in Him. Joy, true joy, can be ours during trials if we realize one fact: we grow through them. If your life is in God's hands, things are not getting worse but better. Trials are for a good and necessary purpose–to make us stronger, more pure and more effective. You can press on if you remember three crucial points:
1. We will have many trials and temptations.
2. We must develop the attitude of joy during trials and temptations.
3. We will be made more perfect and entire through trials and temptations.

PERSONAL JOURNAL NOTES:
(Reflection and Response)

1. The most important thing that I learned from this lesson was:

2. The thing that I need to work on the most is:

3. I can apply this lesson to my life by:

4. Closing Prayer of Commitment:

---

9 Paul Lee Tan. *Encyclopedia of 15,000 Illustrations.* (Rockville, MD: Assurance Publishers, 1988), #14587.

	B. The Way to Conquer Trials & Temptation, 1:5-12	low degree rejoice in that he is exalted: 10 But the rich, in that he is made low: because as the flower of the grass he shall pass away.	status a. Because the poor believer is exalted by Christ b. Because the rich believer is humbled by Christ
1. Ask wisdom of God	5 If any of you lack wisdom, let him ask of God, that giveth to all men liberally, and upbraideth not; and it shall be given him.		
a. God gives generously			1) The rich face a danger: False security
b. God does not scold		11 For the sun is no sooner risen with a burning heat, but it withereth the grass, and the flower thereof falleth, and the grace of the fashion of it perisheth: so also shall the rich man fade away in his ways.	2) The body of the rich ages & dies: Illustrated by the burning heat of the sun
c. Ask in faith, never doubting	6 But let him ask in faith, nothing wavering. For he that wavereth is like a wave of the sea driven with the wind and tossed.		
1) Doubting is illustrated by the waves of the sea			3) The pursuits of the rich fade away
2) Doubting receives nothing	7 For let not that man think that he shall receive any thing of the Lord.	12 Blessed is the man that endureth temptation: for when he is tried, he shall receive the crown of life, which the Lord hath promised to them that love him.	**3. Remember the reward for persevering: A crown of life**
3) Doubting shows instability	8 A double minded man is unstable in all his ways.		
2. Rejoice in your	9 Let the brother of		

Section I
TEMPTATIONS AND TRIALS: THE BASIC FACTS
James 1:2-27

STUDY 2: THE WAY TO CONQUER TRIALS AND TEMPTATION

Text: **James 1:5-12**

Aim: **To develop a strategy for conquering trials and temptations.**

Memory Verse:

> **"Blessed is the man that endureth temptation: for when he is tried, he shall receive the crown of life, which the Lord hath promised to them that love him" (James 1:12).**

INTRODUCTION:
Trials and temptations are common to us all. We all suffer such burdens as…

• pain	• separation	• hurt
• sickness	• divorce	• emptiness
• disease	• disappointment	• loneliness
• death		

And we all face such temptation as…

• immorality	• dishonesty
• greed	• untruthfulness
• lust	• anger

15

The lists could go on and on. What is the worst trial you are facing—right now? What is the worst temptation—the one that swarms in upon you and overcomes you and leads you into sin?

Is there an escape? Is there a way to overcome the trial? the temptation? A way that can assure victory and deliverance? There certainly is, but the way is found only in wisdom from God. You cannot escape temptation by "turning over a new leaf," reading a self-help book, or getting the latest therapy. A person must put all his faith in God in order to conquer temptation. This is the subject of this passage: *The way to conquer trials and temptations*.

OUTLINE:
1. Ask wisdom of God (vv.5-8).
2. Rejoice in your status (vv.9-11).
3. Remember the reward for enduring: a crown of life (v.12).

1. ASK WISDOM OF GOD (vv.5-8)

How can a believer conquer trials and temptations? First, he must ask wisdom of God. Wisdom means far more than just knowledge, far more than just being intellectual about life or some area of life. Knowledge is the grasping of facts, and most people in the world have heads full of facts.

⇒ Just think of all the schools in the world: schools for children, schools for young people, schools for men and women, schools for tradesman.

⇒ Think of the millions of farmers, scientists, business people, tradesmen, mechanics, contractors, physicians, and on and on.

Millions and millions of us are knowledgeable. But when coping with the trials and temptations of life, something more than a head full of facts is needed. Being a knowledgeable person is not enough in order to be a victorious and fulfilled person. Wisdom is what is needed. But what does the Bible mean by wisdom? Wisdom is not only seeing and knowing about life, it is seeing and knowing what to do about life.

Wisdom grasps the great truths of life. It sees the trials and temptations that surround life and death, God and man, time and eternity, good and evil—the deep things of the universe and of God. But wisdom not only grasps these facts, wisdom knows what to do about them, and then does it. Wisdom not only understands the trials and temptations, but it understands how to conquer them and then does it. Wisdom acts and conquers and gains the victory over the trials and temptations.

Now, if we lack that kind of wisdom—if we do not understand, if we do not know how to conquer life or some trial and temptation—then there is one sure way to get the wisdom:

> **"If any of you lack wisdom, let him ask of God...and it shall be given him" (Js.1:5).**

Asking wisdom of God is the way to conquer the trials and temptations of life. Now, note two significant points.

1. Note the wonderful promises made to us when we ask God for wisdom.
    ⇒ God will give us wisdom.
    ⇒ God will give us a liberal amount, an abundance of wisdom.

⇒ God will not reproach or rebuke us—not scold us—for not knowing how to handle the trial or temptation. The idea is that God will not even question us for lacking wisdom and for not knowing what to do.

God loves us; we are His sons and daughters. He is our Father, and He wants to meet our every need. Therefore, God will hear our request and our cry; He will give us the wisdom to conquer the trials and temptations of life.

2. Note a critical fact: we have a responsibility. We must do something, and whether God hears us depends upon our doing this one thing. If we do it, God hears us and gives us wisdom to conquer the trials and temptations. If we do not do it, God cannot hear us. What is it that we must do? When we ask God to give us wisdom to conquer some trial or temptation, *we must ask in faith and not waver*. We must believe that God loves and cares for us, that He will hear our cries and prayers and meet our every need. When we pray and cry out to God, we cannot doubt; that is, we cannot ask and then...

wonder if God really exists
wonder if God is really going to hear
wonder if God can really do what we ask
wonder if we really know God well enough for Him to hear us
wonder if the request is the will of God

Such doubting cannot be heard by God. God cannot answer the prayer of a doubting person. If He did, then He would be rewarding doubt—rewarding those who do not believe or trust Him. He would be rewarding those who ignore, neglect, question and, in many cases, curse, deny, and fight against Him. God cannot hear and answer a person who wavers in his faith. We must believe that God is, that He exists, and that He does love and care for us. We must believe that He will hear and answer us when we ask for wisdom to face the trials and temptations of life.

> **"But without faith it is impossible to please him: for he that cometh to God must believe that he is, and that he is a rewarder of them that diligently seek him" (He.11:6).**

Note what Scripture says about the person who wavers in faith.
a. First, the person is just like a wave of the sea driven by the wind and tossed to and fro.
b. Second, the person will not receive anything of the Lord. Why? Because a person who wavers back and forth does not know the value of God's gifts. If God granted them, the person would not always use them nor would he use the gifts as they should be used. If God gave the wisdom to a person to conquer the trials and temptations of life, the person might or might not use it or might use it irregularly. He might misuse it or abuse it. Therefore, the person who wavers in faith will not receive anything from God.
c. Third, the person who wavers in faith is a double-minded person, and he is unstable in all his ways. A person who wavers in faith lives a life that is up and down, back and forth. His whole behavior, including his prayer life, is unstable and unreliable. He is like a person with two minds: he is not sure; he is uncertain; he feels *yes* and then he feels *no*. He believes, then he disbelieves.

ILLUSTRATION:

> It was a good answer that was once given by a poor woman to a minister
> who asked her, "What is faith?" She replied: "I am ignorant, and I cannot an-
> swer well, but I think it is taking God at His Word."[10]

May the Lord help us to remember this simple and wonderful truth: God is
always true to His Word. What pearls of wisdom!

QUESTIONS:
1. In practical terms, how is wisdom different from knowledge?
2. Why do we need wisdom to be able to conquer trials?
3. Tell about a time when God gave you just the wisdom you needed.
4. What kinds of instability come from not fully trusting in God?

2. REJOICE IN YOUR STATUS (vv.9-11)

How can a believer conquer trials and temptations? The believer must rejoice in his
status in life. Whether a person is poor or rich, healthy or unhealthy, crippled or
sound, he is to rejoice in the Lord.

1. First, the believer of lowly status is to rejoice in the Lord. This does not mean
that he is to rejoice because he is poor, unhealthy, or crippled. It means that he rejoices
in Christ despite the circumstances—no matter how terrible. Christ loves the lowly person. Christ has saved the lowly person and has promised to exalt him as a king and
prince throughout all eternity. Therefore, the believer of lowly status is to have a spirit
that is as strong as the spirit of a king and prince. A lowly person who does not allow
his status to defeat him but, rather, conquers his status develops a strong, strong spirit.
He develops such a strong spirit that with the wisdom of God he can conquer any trial
or temptation thrown against him.

2. Second, the believer of rich or high status in life is to rejoice in that he is made
low by God. What does this mean?

   a. First, a rich or high person is not accepted by God because of who he is or
      what he has. His rich and high status means absolutely nothing to God. Even
      if he were the ruler and owner of the whole earth, it would mean nothing to
      God. What is such status or wealth in comparison to the whole universe? The
      rich and high have to approach God bare—as nothing and as having nothing—
      approach Him as a little child, poor and without anything. This is the only
      way God accepts any person; therefore, the rich and high are no better off
      than the poor and lowly. All men—no matter their status in life—stand before
      God as equals. Let the rich and high rejoice in God and in the fact that God
      accepts him, not in his rich and high status.

   b. Second, a rich and high person must use all that he has and is—all of his
      riches and high influence—to help meet the desperate needs of the starving,
      impoverished, diseased, homeless, sinful, dying, and lost of the world. This is
      a fact that is neglected, ignored, explained away, and in some cases denied.
      Nevertheless, let the Word of God be true and every man a liar—as Scripture
      says. It is the clear teaching of Scripture (see Mt.19:16-22; 19:23-26; 19:27-
      30). The rich and high are to give and live just as sacrificially in meeting the
      needs of the lost and needy of the world as the middle and lower classes of so-
      ciety. They are to use all to meet the desperate needs of this world for the

---

10 Richard A. Steele, Jr. and Evelyn Stoner. *Practical Bible Illustrations from Yesterday and Today.* (Chattanooga, TN: AMG Publishers, 1996), #402.

gospel and for food, water, medicine, education, clothing, and housing. Note what this passage says: the rich and high must remember a critical fact:

"For he remembered that they were but flesh; a wind that passeth away, and cometh not again" (Ps.78:39).

ILLUSTRATION:
How many people—rich or otherwise—when facing death try to bargain with God? How many would trade their wealth for more time?

The famous author, Oscar Wilde, once wisely noted, "No man is rich enough to buy back his past." Truly, we have only one chance to make the most of each day, then it is gone.

QUESTIONS:
1. No matter what our status in life, what should be our attitude toward trials and temptations? What reasons do you have to rejoice today?
2. Why is it important not to seek to exalt ourselves?
3. If any person wants to be accepted by God, what attitude is absolutely necessary?
4. What spiritual good can you do with your earthly possessions?

3. REMEMBER THE REWARD FOR PERSEVERING: A CROWN OF LIFE (v.12)

How can a believer conquer trials and temptations? He must remember the reward for enduring. He will be blessed and will receive a crown of life. Note exactly what is said.

1. The person who endures temptation will be "blessed." The word "blessed" here refers to this life, to the here and now. The word *blessed* refers to inward and spiritual joy and satisfaction; an inner assurance and confidence that carries one through all the trials and temptations of life no matter the pain, sorrow, loss, or grief. Simply stated, the person is secure in this life. He knows that God is looking after and caring for him and is going to deliver him from all the corruption and evil of this life including death, giving him life eternal.

"He is like a man which built an house, and digged deep, and laid the foundation on a rock: and when the flood arose, the stream beat vehemently upon that house, and could not shake it: for it was founded upon a rock." (Lu.6:48).

2. The person will receive the crown of life in the next world. What is the crown of life? *Life itself* is the crown.[11] The believer who endures the temptations of this life will be crowned with eternal life—life that will go on and on, never ending. The eternal life given to the believer will shine more brightly than all the earthly crowns ever worn by the rulers of this world.

APPLICATION:
Just imagine the actual moment when Christ crowns us with the crown of life. Being crowned...
will fill us with unbroken joy and rejoicing
will bestow upon us honor and dignity
will give us a deep and perfect sense of victory and triumph
will conform us to the image of eternal royalty

---

[11] A.T. Robertson. *Word Pictures in the New Testament*, Vol.6, p.17.

"And this is the promise that he hath promised us, even eternal life" (1 Jn.2:25).

3. The person who endures trials and temptations is the person who will be blessed and receive the crown of life. But endurance is an absolute essential. A person has to confront the trials and temptations with the spirit of a conqueror; he has to...

- endure
- persevere
- be steadfast
- stand fast
- carry on
- keep trying
- persist
- stick with it

He has to conquer and triumph through Christ Jesus our Lord, and then he will receive the promises of God. A person has to be tried and tested and has to prove faithful. He has to endure to the end in order to be saved and to inherit the crown of life.

ILLUSTRATION:
What a marvelous reward awaits the genuine believer. The human mind cannot imagine what lies in store. As the Apostle Paul wrote, "Eye hath not see, nor ear heard, neither have entered into the heart of man, the things which God hath prepared for them that love him" (1 Co.2:9). D.L. Moody described heaven this way:

> *The paradise of Eden was as nothing compared with [heaven]. ... Think of a place where temptation cannot come. Think of a place where we will be free from sin; where pollution cannot enter, and where the righteous shall reign forever. Think of a city ... without griefs or graves, without sins or sorrows.* [12]

How beautiful and glorious heaven will be! Do not miss out on your heavenly reward for the corruptible things of this world!

QUESTIONS:
1. What does the Bible mean by the word "blessed" in v.12? What are some examples of these blessings in your life?
2. What temptations are keeping you from receiving the crown of life? What can you do about them?
3. How would you rate your level of endurance? Is it strong enough to survive and overcome to the end?

SUMMARY:

Trials and temptations often flood in upon us. In a weak moment, endurance seems impossible, not to mention victory. Even the Apostle Paul felt this way and prayed he would not go through such experiences. Nevertheless, Paul was assured that God's grace was all he needed to make it through the trial (2 Co.12:9). We have the examples of Paul and many other strong Christians when we face difficult times. But even more important, we have the great example of Christ Himself. And Christ promises to help us whenever we call out to Him. With His help, we can endure any trial, no matter how terrible. Our task is to follow the steps spelled out in this passage:
1. Ask wisdom of God.
2. Rejoice in your status.
3. Remember the reward for enduring: a crown of life.

---

[12] John W. Reed. *1100 Illustrations from the Writings of D. L. Moody.* (Grand Rapids, MI: Baker Books, 1990), p.137.

JAMES 1:5-12

PERSONAL JOURNAL NOTES:
(Reflection and Response)

1. The most important thing that I learned from this lesson was:

2. The thing that I need to work on the most is:

3. I can apply this lesson to my life by:

4. Closing Prayer of Commitment:

	C. The Origin of Trials & Temptation, 1:13-18	and sin, when it is finished, bringeth forth death.	c. The result: Death
1. Temptation is not of God	13 Let no man say when he is tempted, I	16 Do no err, my beloved brethren.	**3. Temptation is not of God's nature**
a. God is never tempted	am tempted of God: for God cannot be	17 Every good gift and every perfect gift	a. God is only good
	tempted with evil,	is from above, and cometh down from	b. God gives only good gifts: He is as unchangeable
b. God tempts no man	neither tempteth he any man:	the Father of lights, with whom is no	as the heavenly lights He created
2. Temptation is of man, of his own lust or evil desire	14 But every man is tempted, when he is drawn away of his	variableness, neither shadow of turning.	(sun, moon, stars)
a. Lust & enticement	own lust, and enticed.	18 Of his own will begat he us with the	c. God wills only to see us born again
b. The conception of lust & the birth of sin	15 Then when lust hath conceived, it bringeth forth sin:	word of truth, that we should be a kind of firstfruits of his creatures.	

Section I
TEMPTATIONS AND TRIALS: THE BASIC FACTS
James 1:2-27

STUDY 3: THE ORIGIN OF TRIALS AND TEMPTATION

Text: **James 1:13-18**

Aim: To know and understand the source of temptation.

Memory Verse:

> **"Let no man say when he is tempted, I am tempted of God: for God cannot be tempted with evil, neither tempteth he any man" (James 1:13).**

INTRODUCTION:
Where does temptation come from? Sometimes the desire or craving for things upon earth is almost unbearable. We see something and know that it is wrong, that we should not have it or do it, yet the desire becomes so strong that we can hardly stand it. The craving may be for things such as...

food	immoral sex
clothing	worldly possessions
cigarettes	recognition or authority
alcohol	position or advancement
pornography	selfish ambition

This is what temptation is: the desire or craving for things that God forbids or that are harmful to our bodies or spirits. No matter what it is—even if man justifies it and says it is acceptable—it is sin if God says it is wrong or if it harms our bodies or spirits. Therefore, when we feel an urge or craving for such things, we are being tempted, and the temptation is to be fled from.

Now, where does temptation come from? Take any of the things mentioned above: Why do we desire and crave them? What causes the urge for them? Knowing the origin of temptation will help us tremendously in conquering the trials and temptations of life.

OUTLINE:
  1. Temptation is not of God (v.13).
  2. Temptation is of man, of his own lust (vv.14-16).
  3. Temptation is not of the nature of God (vv.17-18).

1. TEMPTATION IS NOT OF GOD (v.13).

Man is always blaming someone else for tempting him and leading him into sin. When Adam and Eve fell into sin, God found Adam and asked him what had happened. Adam, trying to escape the blame, did just what all of us are prone to do: he said, "the woman who *you gave me* tempted me" (Ge.3:12). Then when God turned to Eve, Eve said: "the serpent deceived me" (Ge.3:13). The point is this: man seldom takes responsibility for his own wrongdoing.

What we do is try to justify our behavior and quiet our conscience by blaming a family member, spouse, employer, or anyone other than ourselves. But note what we have done: we have blamed God. How?

⇒ By wondering why God ever let such a thing happen to us: such a bad marriage, such a terrible accident, such poor health, and a host of other things.

⇒ By reasoning that God created us with desires and passions; therefore, when we slip here and there, He will understand and forgive us.

⇒ By thinking that God made the world as it is and everything in it; therefore, if we indulge in worldly things, He will understand and forgive us. It may be a second helping or a second drink or a second look at a loosely dressed woman, but we excuse ourselves with the thought that indulgence is understood by God.

God, of course, did create all things in their raw form, and He created us with desires and passions. God created food and He gave us a desire for food so that we would eat and take care of our bodies. God gave man to woman and woman to man so that they would keep the human race going and would build companionship, trust, and family. They would build a world of love, peace, joy, and of worship and service to God. But God did not make us...

• to desire, and then to desire more and more
• to crave, and then to crave more and more

God is not the Person who arouses lustful desires and cravings within us. Note what this verse says:

> **"Let no man say [or think or rationalize, or justify his behavior]**
> **when he is tempted, I am tempted of God" (Js.1:13).**

1. First, God cannot be tempted with evil. God is holy, righteous, and pure. Therefore, by His very nature God can have absolutely nothing to do with evil or temptation. To tempt a person is an evil thing to do. Thus it takes a selfish, carnal, and evil person to try to entice and seduce another person to do the forbidden thing. And God is not like this. God is the very opposite.

2. Second, not only can God not be tempted by evil, but God *does not tempt* any person. God loves, cares for, and seeks to save man, not to damage or destroy man's body and spirit. When a person is tempted to do the forbidden or harmful thing, the urge and craving is not of God. God wants the person to turn away and flee the temptation, not to crumble and succumb to it.

"There hath no temptation taken you but such as is common to man: but God is faithful, who will not suffer you to be tempted above that ye are able; but will with the temptation also make a way to escape, that ye may be able to bear it" (1 Co.10:13).

ILLUSTRATION:
When we sin, we must not look for an excuse or for someone else to blame. The fault lies within each one of us. Consider this:

> *How does a worm get inside an apple? Perhaps you think the worm burrows in from the outside. No, scientists have discovered that the worm comes from the inside. But how does it get in there? Simple. An insect lays an egg in the apple blossom. Sometime later the worm hatches in the heart of the apple, then eats its way out.* [13]

We all have desires within that can damage the beautiful fruit God wants us to produce. We must seek the help of the Holy Spirit to daily overcome our temptation to feed the flesh.

QUESTIONS:
1. How can you avoid blaming others?
2. Why can God never be the source of temptation to do evil?
3. How has God shown you a way out of temptation? What is His will for you in these situations?

2. TEMPTATION IS OF MAN, OF HIS OWN LUST (vv.14-16).

There are three significant steps involved in temptation and sin, three steps that we must understand if we are to consistently conquer temptation.

1. There is lust and enticement. Every man—without exception—is tempted when he is drawn away and enticed by his own lusts. The word "lust" means to crave either good or evil. There are good desires and bad desires. The word "enticed" means to lure and bait just as a person lures and baits a fish.

The picture is this: man has good desires, natural and normal desires. Therefore, when he begins to think about or look at something, he very naturally desires it. His desire is normal behavior. The problem arises when the thing is forbidden or is harmful. If he looks at and thinks about the forbidden or harmful thing, he begins to lust and to be enticed or lured to go after it. This is the very beginning stage of temptation. Man takes his desire and focuses it upon the forbidden or harmful thing. He begins to pay attention to what he should not look at; he begins to think about the things of the flesh and of the world. Thereby he is tempted and drawn away by his own lusts.

2. There is the conception of lust and the birth of sin. The above point, point one, is what is called the conception of lust. It is a picture of birth. When a person actually begins to look at and think about the forbidden thing, desire and lust are *conceived* in his mind. He pictures the pleasure of the desire; that is, sin is actually born. Picturing—looking at or thinking about the desire—is sin.

The point to note is this: temptation begins with the normal and natural desires of man and with his thoughts. A person sees, smells, tastes, hears, touches, or thinks about something—something that is forbidden and harmful—and he fails to turn away and flee from it. It may be something as simple as hearing or listening to suggestive music, music about the intimacy of a relationship. Instead of fleeing, the person allows

---

[13] Ted Kyle and John Todd. *A Treasury of Bible Illustrations*, #771.

his mind to conceive the thing or act. He pictures the pleasure and begins to desire or lust after it. Sin in born; the wrong is committed right there in his mind. His heart is set upon the forbidden thing. He may never do the act, but he would if he had the chance and the courage.

APPLICATION:
The way to overcome temptation is essentially twofold.
1) If the temptation attacks our thoughts, then we must push the wrong thought out of our mind, and then begin immediately to focus our thoughts upon Christ and some passage of Scripture.
2) If the temptation comes from an attraction to our senses—seeing, hearing, tasting, or touching—then we must turn our head or body away and flee the temptation. Then immediately we must focus upon Christ and prayer and review some Scripture passage.

3. There is the result of lust and enticement: death. The basic meaning of death is *separation*. Death never means extinction, annihilation, nonexistence, or inactivity. Man dies physically, spiritually, and eternally because of sin. When God created man, He did not create man to die. Man, through his sin, has chosen to die.

> **"And as it is appointed unto men once to die, but after this the judgment" (He.9:27).**

APPLICATION:
William Barclay has a thought on temptation that should challenge us to turn our total being over to Christ.

> *Now desire is something which can be nourished or stifled. A man can...by the grace of God, eliminate desire if he faces it and deals with it at once. But...*
> * *he can allow his steps to take him into certain places and certain company*
> * *he can encourage his eyes to linger on certain forbidden things*
> * *he can spend his life fomenting desire*
> * *he can use mind and heart and eyes and feet and lips to nourish desire*
>
> *[However, a man] can so hand himself over to Christ and to the Spirit of Christ that he is cleansed of evil desire. He can be so engaged on good things that there is no time or place left for desire. It is idle hands for which Satan finds mischief to do; and it is an unexercised mind which plays with desire, and an uncommitted heart which is vulnerable to the appeal of lust.*
> *If a man nourishes and encourages desire long enough, there is an inevitable consequence. Desire becomes action. If a man thinks about anything long enough if he allows himself to desire it long enough, all the chances are that in the end he will do it. Desire in the heart in the end begets sin in the action.[14]*

ILLUSTRATION:

> *Along the banks of the Amazon River lives a species of large, colorful spiders. When one of these creatures spreads itself out, it looks exactly like the*

---

14 William Barclay. *The Letters of James* and *Peter*. "The Daily Study Bible." (Philadelphia, PA: The Westminster Press, 1958), p.61f. Statements in outline form by us for emphasis.

blossom of a brilliant flower. Bees and other insects lighting upon it expect to find nectar. But instead, the spider secretes a deadly poison. [15]

Sin is very much like that spider. It lures, invites, and even appears to be good for us. But beware: death awaits the person who gives in to the seduction!

QUESTIONS:
1. When does normal desire become sin? How can you avoid crossing over the line between the two?
2. Sin always causes death, separation from God. Does your lifestyle back up your belief in this fact? How can you convey this in practical terms to the unsaved?

3. TEMPTATION IS NOT OF THE NATURE OF GOD (vv.17-18).

Note three significant points about God and temptation.

1. God is good and perfect. He would not be not God if He were not good and perfect. When we say *God*, we mean the Supreme and Majestic Being of the universe, the Being who is the Creator, the Being who is good and perfect—who is the Source of all good and perfect gifts. Being good and perfect, God can have absolutely nothing to do with temptation and sin. Therefore, He is not the one who tempts man. God is the One who gives man every good and perfect gift that man receives.

> **"As for God, his way is perfect: the word of the Lord is tried: he is a buckler [shield] to all those that trust in him" (Ps.18:30).**

2. God is the Father of lights and He is unchangeable. It is temptation that leads men into the world of darkness, the darkness of guilt and shame, of personal disappointment and accusation, of hurting and damaging others, of destruction and death, of secrecy and hidden affairs, of the night and closed doors, of hidden and secret acts. God is the Creator of the sun, moon, and stars and of light itself. He is unchangeable. He always gives us the things that will stand in the light, things…
- that give us joy
- that are good for us
- that do not shame us
- that can build us up and perfect and mature us
- that give us assurance and confidence
- that make us secure
- that bring us love and joy and peace
- that will open up the light of truth
- that will take us out of darkness
- that are good and perfect
- that show forth Christ and God

3. God wills above all else to see us born again. He wills for us to know the Word of truth. If we ever hear words of error, they are not of God. All humanistic and false teaching are not of God. They are of some other source, a source that is out to tempt man away from God and His truth. God wants man to be born again. Man—every man—has been physically born and the way of physical birth is death. Every human being will die. But God's will is what the Word of truth proclaims: that man can be *born*

---

[15] Paul Lee Tan. *Encyclopedia of 15,000 Illustrations,* #13091.

again. He can experience a spiritual rebirth and live forever with God in the new heavens and earth. We can all become one of His new creatures, a *new person* who is going to be perfected and live forever and ever. We can all be like the first fruits of the vine, a new fruit, a new creature that is unlike the physical creature that we are upon this material earth. We can be made into one of God's new creatures—made into perfect beings who will live forever to worship and serve God in the new heavens and earth.

> **"But as many as received him, to them gave he power to become the sons of God, even to them that believe on his name: which were born, not of blood, nor of the will of the flesh, nor of the will of man, but of God" (Jn.1:12-13).**

QUESTIONS:
1. Why is it completely impossible for God to be the source of temptation?
2. How have you found God's gifts to be better than what the world has to offer?
3. How can you avoid the false teachings that tempt you to stray from God?

SUMMARY:

Money, sex, power. We can be sure that Satan will do his best to put these and other temptations before us. He will make them look very attractive. But he cannot entice us to sin unless we take our eyes off the Lord, shift our focus away from the Word of God, the truth. Just like Adam and Eve in the garden giving in to the forbidden fruit, temptation can become sin and grip us before we know it. But we can avoid its evil clutch if we focus on Christ and God's Word, realizing and understanding that:
1. Temptation is not of God.
2. Temptation is of man, of his own lust.
3. Temptation is not of the nature of God.

PERSONAL JOURNAL NOTES:
(Reflection and Response)

1. The most important thing that I learned from this lesson was:

2. The thing that I need to work on the most is:

3. I can apply this lesson to my life by:

4. Closing Prayer of Commitment:

	D. The Preparations Necessary to Withstand Trials & Temptation, 1:19-27	face in a glass: 24 For he beholdeth himself, and goeth his way, and straightway forgetteth what manner of man he was.	
1. Preparation 1: Be quick to hear the Word of God	19 Wherefore, my beloved brethren, let every man be swift to hear, slow to speak, slow to wrath:	25 But whoso looketh into the perfect law of liberty, and continueth therein,	b. A doer of the Word is blessed
a. By being slow to speak	20 For the wrath of man worketh not the righteousness of God.	he being not a forgetful hearer, but a doer of the work, this man shall be blessed in his deed.	
b. By being slow to anger: An angry man does not do what God says, does not live a righteous life	21 Wherefore lay apart all filthiness and superfluity of naughtiness, and receive with meekness the engrafted word, which is able to save your souls.		
c. By putting aside all moral filth		26 If any man among you seem to be religious, and bridleth not his tongue, but deceiveth his own heart, this man's religion is vain.	**3. Preparation 3: Control the tongue**
d. By putting aside all evil			
e. By receiving the Word with humility			
2. Preparation 2: Be a doer of the Word & not a hearer only	22 But be ye doers of the word, and not hearers only, deceiving your own selves.	27 Pure religion and undefiled before God and the Father is this, To visit the fatherless and widows in their affliction, and to keep himself unspotted from the world.	**4. Preparation 4: Practice pure religion—visit the needy & keep yourself from being corrupted by the world**
a. A person who only listens to the Word deceives himself: He soon forgets what he heard	23 For if any be a hearer of the word, and not a doer, he is like unto a man beholding his natural		

Section I
TEMPTATIONS AND TRIALS: THE BASIC FACTS
James 1:2-27

STUDY 4: **THE PREPARATIONS NECESSARY TO WITHSTAND TRIALS AND TEMPTATION**

Text: **James 1:19-27**

Aim: To plant the Word of God so firmly in your heart that you will be prepared for temptation.

Memory Verse:

> **"But be ye doers of the word, and not hearers only, deceiving your own selves" (James 1:22).**

INTRODUCTION:
"Prepare for battle!" How often these words have caused the hearts and minds of soldiers to race. Yet preparation for battle occurs long before the battle actually takes place. Soldiers have to learn how to attack, how to defend, and how to care for their

weapons, each other, and themselves. They have to prepare by doing exactly what they are commanded so that when orders are given on the battlefield, they are quick and exact in their movements.

So it is in our spiritual warfare. There are several preparations that must be made in order to overcome temptation. Without these preparations, temptation can never be conquered.

OUTLINE:
1. Preparation 1: be quick to hear the Word of God (vv.19-21).
2. Preparation 2: be a doer of the Word and not a hearer only (vv.22-25).
3. Preparation 3: control the tongue (v.26).
4. Preparation 4: practice pure religion—visit the needy and keep yourself from being corrupted by the world (v.27).

1. PREPARATION ONE—BE QUICK TO HEAR THE WORD OF GOD (vv.19-21).

The thrust of these three verses is seen in v.21: receiving the Word so that a person's soul will be saved. The greatest temptation in the world is for a person to walk through life doing what he wants and pleases, thereby ignoring, neglecting, and rejecting God. The result of this path is death (Ja.1:15). Therefore, if a person is to be saved—if he is to be delivered from the great temptation that will doom his soul—he must prepare himself. He must be quick to hear the Word of God. How can a person make sure that he hears the Word of God? Make sure that he can receive the Word and save his soul? This passage states that he must do five things.

1. He must be slow to speak. This means that a person must be willing to listen instead of speaking his own ideas about right and wrong and about how a person is saved. He must be willing to listen to God's Word instead of insisting upon what he thinks.

2. He must be slow to wrath or anger. This means at least two things.
   ⇒ A person must not react against what God says about temptation and sin nor about what God says about salvation. If a person reacts against God's plan of salvation and follows his own plan, he is dooming himself. No person can ever be saved or conquer temptation if he reacts in anger against God's Word of salvation and righteousness.
   ⇒ A person must not become angry and act against others in wrath. Anger and wrath disturb and distract. An angry person cannot focus his thoughts and spirit upon God's Word, not enough to hear what the Word is saying. An angry person cannot do what God says; he cannot live righteously nor receive the righteousness of God's salvation (v.20).

3. He must put aside all filthiness. The picture is that of *taking off* a dirty garment and putting it aside. A person must put off every dirty thing and lay it off to the side away from himself. If he enjoys the dirt and filth, then his mind will not be clear, not enough to hear the Word of God. William Barclay makes the point that the word for "filthiness" is sometimes used to refer to *wax in the ear*.[16] The picture is descriptive: a person with wax in the ear cannot hear the Word of God, not clearly. Therefore, he must take the wax out of his ear and put it away or else he will be deaf to the Word of God.

4. He must put aside all that remains of naughtiness, wickedness, and evil. The idea is this: even after putting aside all filthiness, there will still be some naughtiness or

---

16 William Barclay. *The Letters of James and Peter*, p.66.

wickedness that will show up within us. Therefore, we must be alert to these uprisings and put them off or lay them aside as well.

5. He must receive the Word of God with meekness. He must be *as a child* before God our Father, that is, sit before Him meekly just as a child does his father. The idea is that we must be humble, gentle, quiet, and attentive in listening to the Word of God.

Note the word "engrafted" in verse 21. It means to implant; to be born within. When a person listens to and hears the Word of God, the Word is planted within his heart and life. What God says is actually born within his heart, and the person hears exactly what God says. The person's soul is thereby saved, and he conquers and triumphs over all temptation, including the terrible temptation to reject God and live as he wants. He is saved to live eternally with God. The first preparation a person must make to withstand temptation is to be quick to hear the Word of God.

> "But that on the good ground are they, which in an honest and good heart, having heard the word, keep it, and bring forth fruit with patience" (Lu.8:15).

ILLUSTRATION:
We must allow God to test our hearts. We must not only let His Word stir us inside but also let it come alive within us, search us, change us. Jesus described this vital fact with the picture of the Sower and the seed. Consider the important teaching concerning the seed of the Word of God in the following quote:

> *The heart, that is so prone to be deceitful, must first be dealt with. The good seed is only fruitful in a "good and honest heart."*[17]

QUESTIONS:
1. What hinders you from hearing God's Word?
2. What specific things can you do to keep an open heart toward the Word of God?

2. PREPARATION TWO: DO THE WORD OF GOD; DO NOT BE A HEARER ONLY (vv.22-25).

We must live and do the Word of God, not just hear it. Note three points.

1. The person who only hears and knows the Word deceives himself. If a person thinks that he can hear and learn the Word of God and then go out and live as he wants, he deceives himself.

APPLICATION:
There are many who sit under the Word of God week after week, and they learn and know as much of the Word as anyone. They think that their listening and learning makes them acceptable to God, that it makes them safe and secure. When they slip into sin, they feel that they can ask God for forgiveness and that He will forgive them. They feel that God would never reject them. But note something, the most critical fact: God does not accept us because we hear and know the Word nor because we confess our sins. Each of these are necessary and very important, but they are not enough.

⇒ God accepts us because we *confess and repent*. Repentance means that we turn away from our sins and turn to God. God accepts us because we turn to Him and live for Him. When we believe God—really believe Him—then we trust and follow Him, doing exactly what He says.

---

[17] James Smith. *Handfuls on Purpose*, 10 vols. (Grand Rapids, MI: Eerdmans Publishing Co., 1947), 7:108.

2. The person who only hears and knows the Word soon forgets what he has heard. If a person does not practice what he learns, it soon fades from memory. It is simply forgotten, and it never becomes a part of the person's life. He is like the person who looks in a mirror to see if he needs to do anything to his appearance, but walks away and thinks of something else.

APPLICATION:
How much like what happens so often. We hear the Word and are convicted of some defect, some shortcoming, some failure that we need to clean up. But as soon as we walk out from under the Word, we are distracted by the world and its affairs and we soon forget to do what the Word of God told us to do—what God Himself has told us to do.

3. The person who obeys and does the Word of God is blessed. Note that the Word of God is called the *perfect law of liberty*. This means that the Word of God will set a person free from the bondages of sin and death. The Word of God will free a person from all the temptations of this life and give him the full and victorious life for which his soul longs—a life that will continue on and on eternally with God.

A person who obeys and lives the Word of God will find that he is freed from all that enslaves his soul upon earth. He will discover love, joy, and peace—a soul that soars with a sense of...

- freedom and liberty
- purpose and meaning
- security and safety
- victory over temptation
- joy and rejoicing
- assurance and confidence
- life over death
- deliverance from sin

> **"For not the hearers of the law are just before God, but the doers of the law shall be justified" (Ro.2:13).**

ILLUSTRATION:
Our obedience to God's Word must follow our hearing it. Without obedience, any attempt to be religious is worthless.

The story is told of two believers discussing how wonderful it would be to tour the Holy Land. This was their conversation:

Believer 1: "Wouldn't it be fantastic to go to the Holy Land, stand on top of Mt. Sinai, and shout out the Ten Commandments right from the very mountain where Moses received them?"
Believer 2: "Yes, it sure would. But do you know what would be even better?"
Believer 1: "What's that?"
Believer 2: "If we kept them."[18]

God does not expect us to be perfect, but He does expect us to be faithful.

QUESTIONS:
1. What are some practical ways you can be a doer of the Word?
2. Why is repentance such a necessary step in doing God's Word?
3. How has obeying God's Word been a source of real freedom for you?

---

[18] Based on Michael P. Green's *1500 Illustrations for Biblical Preaching*. (Grand Rapids, MI: Baker Books, 1989), #984.

3. PREPARATION THREE: CONTROL THE TONGUE (v.26).

If a person thinks that he is religious, that is, acceptable to God, and he does not bridle his tongue, he deceives himself. No matter what he thinks or professes, his religion is empty. The person may be active and very faithful in his religious worship and service, but he is loose with his tongue...

- interrupting and dominating the conversation
- being easily provoked and lashing out at others
- gossiping and telling tales
- criticizing and murmuring
- judging and condemning others
- using slang and cursing
- engaging in suggestive and off-colored talk

As stated, no matter what a person thinks—no matter how religious he is—if he does not bridle his tongue, he deceives himself. His religion is empty. He does not please God and is thereby unacceptable to God. For a person to withstand and to conquer temptation, he must bridle his tongue. This is the third preparation necessary to conquer temptations.

> **"Whoso keepeth his mouth and his tongue, keepeth his soul from troubles" (Pr.21:23).**

QUESTIONS:
1. Why must the Christian believer in particular control his tongue?
2. In what kinds of situation do you have trouble controlling your tongue? How can you overcome the temptation to speak unwisely?

4. PREPARATION FOUR: PRACTICE PURE RELIGION—VISIT THE NEEDY AND KEEP YOURSELF FROM BEING CORRUPTED BY THE WORLD (v.27).

Two things are said to be necessary in this preparation.
1. A person must visit the fatherless and widows in their affliction. This certainly would apply to visiting all who have need within a community, those who are...

- orphaned
- widowed
- shut-in
- newcomers
- lost or unsaved
- fatherless or motherless
- bedridden
- lonely
- grieved

Whatever their need, God expects us to visit them. He expects us to reach our community. Letting the community know that one really cares will cause many to call upon the believers of the church when the hour of crisis strikes, and it will strike, for it strikes us all. In addition to this, every church should, of course, have genuine believers who can share Christ with the lost.

2. A person must keep himself unspotted from the world. Pure religion does not become corrupted with false beliefs or with false religion. It holds to the purity of the gospel and to the Word of God. Pure religion focuses upon the power of God to change lives eternally and it reaches out to change people's lives by visiting them.

Pure religion does not become morally corrupt; it does not become entangled with the affairs and pleasures of this world. True religion stirs people to separate themselves from the things of this world that arouse their fleshly desires and cravings. This is a necessary preparation if a person is to conquer the temptations and sins of this world.

> **"Blessed are the pure in heart: for they shall see God" (Mt.5:8).**

ILLUSTRATION:

There is an old quote that says, "Quite often when a man thinks his mind is getting broader, it's only his conscience stretching." Listen to the pointed words of one mother's son as he describes it further:

> *A mother was helping her son one day with his spelling assignment and they came to the words conscious and conscience. She asked her son, "Do you know the difference between these two words?"*
>
> *He immediately replied, "Sure, Mom. Conscious is when you are aware of something. And conscience is when you wish you weren't."*[19]

If we are to keep ourselves pure, we must listen to the warnings of the Holy Spirit and not allow the world to corrupt us.

QUESTIONS:

1. In everyday society, what does it mean to have pure religion? To truly minister to others?
2. Whose life can you touch today with a caring visit? A helping hand?

SUMMARY:

We must be prepared for trials and temptations. It is not a question of *whether* trials will come; it is only a matter of *when* they will come. That is one reason the Word of God is so important in helping us to stand true during times of testing.

As believers, we should be glad to hear the Word of God. We should accept it with great joy and treasure it in our hearts. After all, the same Word that saved us from sin has the power to keep us from sin. But we must apply it to our hearts so that we will be prepared to fight temptation. We must do four things: We must:

1. Be quick to hear the Word of God.
2. Be a doer of the Word and not a hearer only.
3. Control the tongue.
4. Practice pure religion—visit the needy and keep ourselves from being corrupted by the world.

PERSONAL JOURNAL NOTES:
(Reflection and Response)

1. The most important thing that I learned from this lesson was:

2. The thing that I need to work on the most is:

3. I can apply this lesson to my life by:

4. Closing Prayer of Commitment:

---

[19] *God's Little Devotional Book.* (Tulsa, OK: Honor Books, Inc., 1995), pp.280-81.

CHAPTER 2

II. TEMPTATIONS & TRIALS: COMMON TO ALL CHRISTIAN BELIEVERS, 2:1-26

A. Temptation 1: Showing Partiality & Favoritism, 2:1-13

1. The charge against showing partiality

My brethren, have not the faith of our Lord Jesus Christ, the Lord of glory, with respect of persons.

2. The picture of partiality: Two unbelieving church visitors
  a. One rich—one poor

  b. Partiality shown to the rich

  c. Prejudice shown to the poor

3. The wrong of partiality
  a. It sets one up as a judge
  b. It reveals evil thoughts
  c. It discriminates against the poor: A people especially loved by God

2 For if there come unto your assembly a man with a gold ring, in goodly apparel, and there come in also a poor man in vile raiment;
3 And ye have respect to him that weareth the gay clothing, and say unto him, Sit thou here in a good place; and say to the poor, Stand thou there, or sit here under my footstool:
4 Are ye not then partial in yourselves, and are become judges of evil thoughts?
5 Hearken, my beloved brethren, Hath not God chosen the poor of this world rich in faith, and heirs of the kingdom which he hath promised to them that love him?
6 But ye have despised the poor, Do not rich men oppress you, and draw you before the judgment seats?
7 Do not they blaspheme that worthy name by the which ye are called?
8 If ye fulfil the royal law according to the scripture, Thou shalt love thy neighbour as thyself, ye do well:
9 But if ye have respect to persons, ye commit sin, and are convinced of the law as transgressors.
10 For whosoever shall keep the whole law, and yet offend in one point, he is guilty of all.
11 For he that said, Do not commit adultery, said also, Do not kill. Now if thou commit no adultery, yet if thou kill, thou art become a transgressor of the law.
12 So speak ye, and so do, as they that shall be judged by the law of liberty.
13 For he shall have judgment without mercy, that hath showed no mercy; and mercy rejoiceth against judgment.

  d. It shows an insulting, disgraceful attitude

  e. It shows foolish behavior: It honors those who are oppressive & who slander the name of Christ

4. The warning against partiality
  a. It is sin; it violates the royal law of love
  b. It makes one guilty of the whole law

  c. It is just as serious as adultery and murder

5. The motivation to avoid partiality
  a. We will be judged
  b. We will receive exactly what we have done: A reciprocal judgment, reaping what we sow

---

Section II
TEMPTATIONS AND TRIALS: COMMON TO ALL CHRISTIAN BELIEVERS
James 2:1-26

STUDY 1: TEMPTATION 1: SHOWING PARTIALITY AND FAVORITISM

Text: James 2:1-13

Aim: To make a strong determination: to show love equally to everyone in the church.

Memory Verse:

> "If ye fulfil the royal law according to the scripture, Thou shalt love thy neighbour as thyself, ye do well:" (James 2:8).

INTRODUCTION:

In chapters two and three, James discusses various temptations and trials common to all believers. One of the strongest temptations—and one of the most destructive sins in human history—is that of showing partiality or favoritism to one person while discriminating against another person or even a whole group of people.

How many times have we:

⇒   seen tattered or dirty clothing and avoided a person?

⇒   heard poor speech and considered the person not worth listening to?

⇒   looked at a handicapped person and thought that he or she could not contribute anything worthwhile to the church or to society?

⇒   judged a person because of skin color or nationality?

⇒   excluded certain people from a party or social gathering?

⇒   condemned a person based on rumor or gossip?

⇒   considered ourselves better than other individuals?

Such actions must not be allowed within the church and among believers. We must avoid partiality and favoritism at all costs. James paints a very strong picture—a convicting picture—of an all too common scenario in the church. And we must take his words very seriously.

OUTLINE:

1. The charge against showing partiality (v.1).
2. The picture of partiality: two unbelieving church visitors (vv.2-3).
3. The wrong of partiality (vv.4-7).
4. The warning against partiality (vv.8-11).
5. The motivation to avoid partiality (vv.12-13).

1.   THE CHARGE AGAINST SHOWING PARTIALITY (v.1).

What does it mean to show partiality? It means to favor some people over others or to pay special attention to a person because of his wealth, social standing, position, authority, popularity, looks, or influence. Note that this charge is given to believers...

• to brothers

• to those who have faith in our Lord Jesus Christ who is the Lord of glory

Of all people upon earth, the very people who should not show partiality are believers. The reason is clearly stated in verse one.

1. Everyone who is in the church is a brother—everyone stands on an equal footing before the Lord Jesus Christ. Wealth, status, social standing, position, appearance—nothing matters except all men coming to the Lord Jesus Christ and worshipping Him.

2. Everyone who has faith in our Lord Jesus Christ bows before Him as Lord. This means that the person bows before Christ as a servant or slave. We all come to Him on

an equal footing; no one is higher or more acceptable than anyone else. All are His servants or slaves. Note exactly who Jesus Christ is: He is *the Lord of glory*.

⇒ Jesus Christ is the Lord who rules and reigns in glory, majesty, perfection, dominion, and power. The person who believes and worships the Lord of glory, no matter his status, realizes that he is as all men, as nothing. Therefore, he does not elevate himself nor anyone else above other people, no matter how poor or lowly they may be.

⇒ Jesus Christ is the Lord who left the glory of heaven to come to this corruptible world to save all men. All believers must do just what the Lord of glory did: humble themselves and reach out to bring all men to the Lord Jesus Christ so that they might be saved—reach out to the poor and lowly as well as to the rich and high.

The charge is clear: believers—those who truly believe in the Lord Jesus Christ, the Lord of glory—are not to show partiality or favoritism. It is strictly forbidden.

> **"I charge thee before God, and the Lord Jesus Christ, and the elect angels, that thou observe these things without preferring one before another, doing nothing by partiality" (1 Ti.5:21).**

ILLUSTRATION:
We must never favor one Christian brother or sister over another. Everyone in the church must work together, each one showing the love of Christ, helping to meet each other's needs.

> *A farmer was feeding his animals one day when he noticed one of the recently born piglets was a little smaller than the others. The large piglets were contentedly feeding from the sow. But when the smaller pig tried to get some milk, it was pushed aside by the mother.*
>
> *After two days of this, the larger piglets also pushed aside the runt pig. As the farmer was feeling sorry for the little piglet, he could not help but make a comparison to the church. "Church people can act just like pigs," he mused, "shoving aside those who are treated with contempt by the world." Then he wisely prayed that the lesson God had brought him would be planted firmly in his own heart. "Dear Lord, help me not to be like the pigs. Help me to love those who are hurting and feeling alone. Help me to care about their needs."*

QUESTIONS:
1. What really gives a person status with God?
2. What should be our attitude toward the poor? Toward the rich? What do you need to change to be more consistent in your attitude toward others?
3. Whom do you need to act more kindly toward in your church? How can you do that this week?

2. THE PICTURE OF PARTIALITY: TWO UNBELIEVING CHURCH VISITORS (vv.2-3).

There must be no misunderstanding about what is meant by partiality. Two unbelievers visit the church. One man is sharply dressed, so much so that it is immediately noticed that he is somewhat wealthy. He has on the finest of clothes and an expensive gold ring. The other man is shabbily dressed, and it is immediately noticed that he is very poor. The clothing he is wearing is filthy and worn. The man is so poor that he is actually a dirty, smelly beggar.

The point is this: What happens when these two men visit the church? The picture painted by Scripture is that of showing partiality to the rich man. The rich man is escorted to a good seat. But the poor man is told to stand or be seated away from everyone else at the footstool.

APPLICATION:
Note that the two men represent the extreme ends of wealth and poverty. If partiality is not to be shown in this case, then it is never to be shown. How often has a poor person visited a church and not been welcomed with open arms? How many of us...
- have felt uncomfortable and uneasy around him?
- have ignored, neglected, and shunned him?
- have failed to greet and welcome him?

This is not of Christ. It is wrong.

> **"Defend the poor and fatherless: do justice to the afflicted and needy" (Ps.82:3).**

QUESTIONS:
1. What does it mean to show partiality? In what situations are you tempted to show favoritism?
2. If someone is shunned in your church, how do you think that person is going to react? How would *you* react?
3. Who in your church seems to be less accepted than others? What can you do to correct the situation?

3. THE WRONG OF PARTIALITY (vv.4-7).

There are five things wrong with showing partiality and favoritism.

1. Showing partiality sets one up as the judge of men (v.4). It makes one as God; it says who can worship God and who cannot, who is acceptable to God and who is not. Only God Himself can determine whom He will or will not accept.

2. Showing partiality reveals evil thoughts (v.4). The person who shows partiality focuses upon mundane and changeable things. Such thoughts are corrupt because they focus upon corruptible things and neglect the person entirely. It says that material things such as clothes are more important than the person himself. This, of course, is foolishness. Yet it is exactly how most people behave, for most people in the world do show partiality.

Believers are never to show partiality, not to a single soul. We are to look at the person himself. What matters is his life, his health and soul, his body and spirit. What matters is that he be saved and come to know the love, joy, and peace that only Christ can bring.

3. Showing partiality discriminates against the poor and lowly, a people who are loved by God (v.5). This verse is not saying that God does not love and care for the rich and high. He does, but He also cares for and loves the poor and lowly. Believers are not to shun them nor shut them out of the church.

> **"I know that the LORD will maintain the cause of the afflicted, and the right of the poor" (Ps.140:12).**

4. Showing partiality shows a disgraceful attitude (v.6a). It dishonors, humiliates, shames, disgraces, and insults the poor and lowly person. Just think of the hurt and

pain within the heart of the person who is publicly discriminated against—the pain and hurt when he sees us shun, bypass, ignore, and withdraw from him. No believer is ever to make a person feel unwelcome or of little value and worth.

5. Showing partiality shows foolish behavior (vv.6b-7). Two things are said about the rich that need to be heeded.

⇒ The rich and high usually oppress the poor and they readily grab what they can, using the very laws of the land to do it. The idea is that they use the law unjustly in order to protect and increase their wealth and power.

⇒ The rich and high usually blaspheme the name of Christ. They blaspheme His name by denying, mocking, ridiculing, persecuting, neglecting, ignoring, and rejecting Him as the Savior of the world.

The point is this: Why would the church and its believers show partiality to such people over the poor of the earth? There is no question, a list of sins could be drawn up and discussed about the poor as well. But why show partiality to the rich who are the very ones who oppress the needy of the world? The church and its believers are not to discriminate and show partiality or favoritism to anyone.

"**Blessed is he that considereth the poor: the LORD will deliver him in time of trouble" (Ps.41:1).**

ILLUSTRATION:

How can you better show Christ's love to everyone without partiality? By truly caring about the souls of people. Listen to this terrific example of what one pastor did:

A pastor was praying about the lack of growth in his church. He was deeply burdened about it. The Lord answered him saying, "I love sinners too much to send them to your church."

After much prayer and repentance, the pastor began to seek out sinners in the community. These people soon began asking him spiritual questions, looking for direction. The pastor invited one of these couples to church.

Though the couple had never been to church, they came one Sunday morning because they felt the pastor's genuine concern. But the awful truth about his congregation was quickly demonstrated. Two of the deacons who had been busily seating people now whispered, "Pastor, two people have come into our church and, well, we don't know what to do. The lady has on a very short dress and the man looks like a rough character."

The pastor went to see. There was the couple he had invited. To the surprise of the deacons, the pastor was truly glad to see them. He said to the couple, "Come with me. You will be my special guests today. Sit right here on the front row. And after church, please come to my home. My wife has prepared a good meal." The couple was saved that very service!

May God help each one of us to have this attitude!

QUESTIONS:

1. What foolish sins are at the root of partiality? In which of these areas do you have room for improvement?
2. Think of an instance when a poor or lowly person was shunned in society. What happened? How should the situation have been handled?
3. Why are the rich viewed as *better* than the poor in most societies? How can you prevent yourself from having this dangerous attitude?

4. THE WARNING AGAINST PARTIALITY (vv.8-11).

There are three warnings.
1. Showing partiality is sin; it violates the royal law of love (vv.8-9). The great law of God is the law of love:

"Thou shalt love thy neighbor as thyself" (Le.19:18; see Lu.10:29-37).

Note how important this law is: it is said to be the great "royal law according to the Scripture." It is royal for at least three reasons.
   a. It is the royal law of God's kingdom. It was given by God Himself and reinforced by His Son, the Lord Jesus Christ, when He came to earth.
   b. It is the great law that embraces or includes all other laws. That is, if a person loves God and loves his neighbor as himself, he will automatically be obeying all the other laws.

   "For all the law is fulfilled in one word, even in this; Thou shalt love thy neighbour as thyself" (Ga.5:14).

   c. It is the very commandment that leads to eternal life.

   "Beloved, let us love one other: for love is of God; and every one that loveth is born of God, and knoweth God. He that loveth not knoweth not God; for God is love." (1 Jn.4:7-8).

The point is this: believers are to love people, not show partiality, discriminating against some. Showing partiality is sin and it makes us transgressors of the law.
2. Showing partiality makes a person guilty of the whole law of God (v.10). How is this possible? How can a person be guilty of all the law if he breaks only one law? Men follow God or else they do not follow God. There is no such thing as subtracting the laws that one does not like and keeping the laws that one does like. Every law has been given by God. They all form a whole pattern, a complete style of life. They are all necessary to point one in the right direction and toward the right goal. Thus, to offend in one point or to slip from one law makes one short of the goal.
This is significant for us to notice and heed, for it means...
   • that we cannot pick and choose what laws we will keep and what laws we will violate.
   • that we cannot build up a merit system with God by keeping most of the laws and be allowed to break a few of the laws.
   • that we cannot become more acceptable to God because we keep most of the laws and break only a few.
   • that we are not more righteous than other people because we keep more laws than they do and break fewer of what men call the more meaningful laws.

The point is this: showing partiality makes a person a terrible law-breaker, the most serious offender imaginable.
3. Showing partiality is just as serious a sin as adultery and killing (v.11). This is an example of what has just been said. But note: the verse may also be saying that partiality is *equal to murder*. Partiality is a sin that selects and favors one person over another. It ignores and neglects another person. It casts him into oblivion, wipes him out; treats him as though he were nothing, absent, or non-existent. Thus, it is comparable to murder. It is the same root, the same cause, the same selfishness, the same lust, the same sin as killing.

This stresses the seriousness of showing partiality. Scripture is clear in its warning: the church and believers are not to show partiality or favoritism to anyone. We are to love all people no matter their social standing or wealth.

QUESTIONS:
1. What one law is critical to the Christian life? What are some practical ways you can love the unlovely this week and avoid the sin of partiality?
2. Discuss why partiality is such a serious sin. What other commands are broken by showing partiality?

5. THE MOTIVATION TO AVOID PARTIALITY (v. 12-13).

There are two things that should stir us to love and care for all people, showing no favoritism whatsoever.

1. We will face the judgment of God (v.12). Therefore, we should *speak and act* like people who will stand before God to give account for what we have done.
   ⇒ We should speak love and kindness to all people.
   ⇒ We should do or show love and kindness to all people.

Who a person is—his social standing and wealth, clothing and appearance—is to have no effect upon us whatsoever. We are to receive people, actually reach out to them through our speech and behavior, no matter who they are. God is going to judge us on the basis of how we have loved and reached out to people, regardless of their status or appearance.

2. We will receive a reward for our behavior. God is going to treat us exactly as we have treated others. If we have shown mercy, then He will show mercy to us; if we have not shown mercy, then He will not show mercy to us. And note: there is only one thing that will be victorious over judgment and that is mercy. Therefore, we must be merciful in order to escape the terrible judgment of God.

> **"For if ye forgive men their trespasses, your heavenly Father will also forgive you: but if ye forgive not men their trespasses, neither will your Father forgive your trespasses" (Mt.6:14-15).**

ILLUSTRATION:

> *The story is told of a scorpion wanting to cross a river. Since he could not swim, he asked the fox to carry him on his back. The fox was not willing at first, because of the threat of the scorpion's sting. But the scorpion said, "Why would I sting you? That would drown both of us." The fox agreed to carry the scorpion, but the scorpion did sting the fox midstream. The fox chided the scorpion, saying, "You foolish creature; now we will both die. Why?" The scorpion only replied, "It's my nature."*—SOURCE UNKNOWN

Because the scorpion did not show mercy, he brought about his own death. Likewise, believers, when they do not show mercy to others, bring about their own ruin. May God help us to have His merciful nature and to show it to others at the needed hour. We must love and care for all people, showing no favoritism whatever.

QUESTIONS:

1. What will God consider important when He judges Christians? What motivates you to show Christian love to people? Do you think you will receive a reward or condemnation for how you have treated others?

2. Why does God require us to show mercy? Whom do you have trouble showing mercy to? How can you improve in this area?

SUMMARY:

The Apostle John in his first epistle had some very strong words to say. He said that if anyone says that he loves God, but hates his brother, then that person is a liar. We simply cannot hate our brother, whom we can see, and love God, Who is invisible (1 Jn. 4:20). Partiality is more than serious; it has eternal consequences. No one can be a Christian believer if he ignores the words of James in today's passage. We simply must heed:

1. The charge against showing partiality.
2. The picture of partiality: two unbelieving church visitors.
3. The wrong of partiality.
4. The warning against partiality.
5. The motivation to avoid partiality.

PERSONAL JOURNAL NOTES:
(Reflection and Response)

1. The most important thing that I learned from this lesson was:

2. The thing that I need to work on the most is:

3. I can apply this lesson to my life by:

4. Closing Prayer of Commitment:

	B. Temptation 2: Professing Faith Without Works, 2:14-26		
		tremble	& shudder
		20 But wilt thou know, O vain man, that faith without works is dead?	b. Conclusion: Faith without works is an empty faith
1. Two basic questions	14 What doth it profit, my breth-ren, though a man say he hath faith, and have not works? can faith save him?	21 Was not Abraham our father justified by works, when he had offered Isaac his son upon the altar?	5. The man who proved his faith by works: Abraham
a. Can a man have faith & not do good works?			a. He offered up Isaac
b. Can faith without good works save a man?			
		22 Seest thou how faith wrought with his works, and by works was faith made perfect?	b. His faith & works were interactive, working together
2. The professing be-liever who is un-concerned & ne-glectful	15 If a brother or sis-ter be naked, and destitute of daily food,		
a. He claims faith, yet refuses to help the needy	16 And one of you say unto them, De-part in peace, be ye warmed and filled; notwithstanding ye give them not those things which are needful to the body; what doth it profit?	23 And the scripture was fulfilled which saith, Abraham be-lieved God, and it was imputed unto him for righteous-ness: and he was called the Friend of God.	c. His faith fulfilled Scripture: He be-lieved God & God credited righteousness to him, to his ac-count
b. Conclusion: His faith without works is dead	17 Even so faith, if it hath not works, is dead, being alone.	24 Ye see then how that by works a man is justified, and not by faith only.	d. Conclusion: A person is justified by faith, proven by his works
3. The two men of ar-rogance	18 Yea, a man may say, Thou hast faith, and I have works: show me thy faith without thy works, and I will show thee my faith by my works.	25 Likewise also was not Rahab the harlot justified by works, when she had re-ceived the messen-gers, and had sent them out another way?	6. The woman who proved her faith by works: Rahab
a. One claims faith; another claims works			a. She proved her faith by receiving & helping the mes-sengers
b. Conclusion: One's faith is shown by works			
4. The orthodox relig-ionist	19 Thou believest that there is one God; thou doest well: the devils also believe, and	26 For as the body without the spirit is dead, so faith with-out works is dead also.	b. Conclusion: A body without the Spirit is dead; so faith without works is dead
a. He believes in one God, but the de-mons also believe			

Section II
TEMPTATIONS AND TRIALS: COMMON TO ALL CHRISTIAN BELIEVERS
James 2:1-26

STUDY 2: TEMPTATION 2: PROFESSING FAITH WITHOUT WORKS

Text: **James 2:14-26**

Aim: To determine the genuineness of your faith by examining your works.

JAMES 2:14-26

Memory Verse:

> **"For as the body without the spirit is dead, so faith without works is dead also" (James 2:26).**

INTRODUCTION:

What is the word of a person worth? Simply this: only what his actions back up. No person can guarantee what he says. Only God can do that. Therefore, the faith that a person professes is only as strong as his works, which are seen outwardly. No matter how nicely we present our faith vocally, no matter how correct our doctrine, it is our actions that demonstrate just how alive our faith really is. This is an inescapable fact.

The greatest tragedy of the church today is the number of people who profess Christ but do not live for Him. Millions profess to be Christians and are baptized, confirmed, or made members of a church; but they do not follow nor live for Christ. They do not live pure and righteous lives, nor do they give all they are and have to reach the lost and needy of the world. Are they saved? Do they have a genuine faith? This is the discussion of this passage. This is the second temptation that is common to all Christian believers: the temptation to profess faith without works.

OUTLINE:

1. Two basic questions (v.14).
2. The professing believer who is unconcerned and neglectful (vv.15-17).
3. The two men of arrogance (v.18).
4. The orthodox religionist (vv.19-20).
5. The man who proved his faith by works: Abraham (vv.21-24).
6. The woman who proved her faith by works: Rahab (vv.25-26).

1. TWO BASIC QUESTIONS (v.14).

There are two questions that every believer needs to ask himself:

⇒ Can a man have faith and not do good works?
⇒ Can faith without good works save a man?

Every thinking person who is honest knows that the answer to these two questions is an emphatic, "No!" A person who really believes something does something; he acts. Nevertheless, millions profess faith in Christ and belong to a church, yet they go on and live like everyone else in the world. Tragically, there is little if any difference in their behavior or speech from the rest of society.

James asks a piercing question: "What profit is it if a man says he has faith, and he does not do good works? Can his faith save him?" Note two significant facts.

1. The man *says* he has faith. But it is *only words*; he does nothing to show that he really believes in Christ. He does not live for Christ; he does not live righteously and godly in this present world, looking for the glorious appearing of the great God and our Savior, Jesus Christ. His faith is only one of profession, not of behavior and life. Note verse 17 and you will see what Scripture calls his faith: a *dead faith*.

2. Note that it is called a *dead faith* three times in this passage (Js.2:17, 20, 26). The faith of a false profession is *vain, empty, unprofitable*—a faith that profits absolutely nothing. It is not enough to claim that we have faith and then not live for Christ. We must truly believe Christ—that He is the Savior and Lord of life. And if we truly believe, we will do what He says. We will live for Him and do the works that please Him. We will live *Christ-centered lives, not self-centered lives*. Five examples follow to illustrate the point.

QUESTIONS:
1. How easily could a person distinguish between your actions and those of an unbeliever? What evidence could the person use to "convict" you of being a Christian?
2. Why is faith without action dead? How is your faith demonstrated by your actions?
3. Describe what it means to live a Christ-centered life on a day-to-day basis.

2. THE PROFESSING BELIEVER WHO IS UNCONCERNED AND NEGLECTFUL (vv.15-17).

There is the example of a destitute Christian believer. This example strongly rebukes us, rebukes most believers and most churches throughout the world. And note: the example is dealing with believers, with brothers and sisters in the Lord.

A brother or sister faces some need or problem that makes him destitute. He is unable to properly dress himself, to stay warm, or to secure enough daily food. We see him and share words of comfort with him. We speak peace and sometimes give a few items to help as he seeks to take care of his most basic needs.

Most believers and churches will go this far. When brothers or sisters have a need, we will visit, comfort, and wish them well. But this is not enough. What good is it if we do not *give them the things they need?*

The point is this: faith, if it does not do good works, is dead. True faith loves and cares and is compassionate in reaching out to help the needy. A person can talk repeatedly about believing in Jesus Christ, but if he is not reaching out to help the destitute of the world as Jesus did, his faith is dead—utterly meaningless. If we really believe in Christ, we will follow Christ: we will take all that *we are and have* beyond our own needs and give it to meet the needs of destitute brothers and sisters.

> **"And he said to them all, If any man will come after me, let him deny himself, and take up his cross daily, and follow me" (Lu.9:23).**

ILLUSTRATION:
Horace Mann, the great educator of the 1800s, once quipped that he had never heard anything about the *resolutions* of the apostles, but he had heard much about the *acts* of the Apostles.

> *An old legend tells about a monk who saw a vision of the Lord. He was so happy, but just then someone knocked on his door and asked for his help. He hesitated, but went to assist his brother. When he returned, Jesus was still there and said, "Had you tarried, I would have gone."*[20]

What a clear statement of God's expectations! We must put our faith into action, reaching out to others, caring about their needs as well as our own.

QUESTIONS:
1. How will someone with true faith respond to a brother or sister in need? Why are words of encouragement not enough?
2. How can you use your resources to help someone in need?

---

[20] Paul Lee Tan. *Encyclopedia of 15,000 Illustrations*, #3401.

3. THERE IS THE EXAMPLE OF TWO MEN OF ARROGANCE (v.18).

James is painting the picture of two men, but only one man speaks and what he says is only one sentence. The speaker says "You have faith and I have works." The picture is that of two arrogant men.

⇒ The man being spoken to has faith. He believes that he is saved by faith—that God accepts him because he believes in Jesus Christ even if he fails to live for Christ. He believes God has accepted him and will take him to heaven when he dies because he has professed Christ, been baptized, and joined the church.

> **"They profess that they know God; but in works they deny him, being abominable, and disobedient, and unto every good work reprobate" (Tit.1:16).**

⇒ The man speaking claims to have works—claims that God accepts him because he does good works and lives as good a life as he can. He believes that the important thing to God is to be religious and do all the good that a person can. If a person does this, God will never reject him; God will accept him no matter who he is and no matter what religion he follows.

> **"Many will say to me in that day, Lord, Lord, have we not prophesied in thy name? and in thy name have cast our devils? and in thy name done many wonderful works?" (Mt.7:22).**

Note that James pulls no punches: it is not a matter of faith or works. To say and profess faith alone will not save a person, and to follow works to become acceptable to God will not save a person. James handles both men of arrogance with one clear statement: "Show me your faith without your works, and I will show you my faith *by my works*."

A person who truly believes in Christ works for Christ. He follows and lives for Christ. A person who only professes Christ lives for himself, going about doing what he wants when he wants. He does not live a life of separation from the world, a life of righteousness and purity, nor does he give all he has to meet the desperate needs of this world. He professes Christ but lives for the pleasures and things of this world.

QUESTIONS:
1. Note the two pictures of arrogance James paints in this passage. Which one is the bigger temptation for you? How can you overcome this temptation?
2. Think for a moment. What evidence in your life shows that you are following Christ?

4. THE ORTHODOX RELIGIONIST (vv.19-20).

There is the example of the orthodox religionists. A true man of religion believes in one God: he is not an atheist or an agnostic nor does he believe in many gods. He is a believer, and note: his belief in God is said to be a good thing. The man does well to believe in God. But there is a *dead belief and a living belief*, a belief that does not lead to salvation, a belief that does lead to salvation.

⇒ Consider the demons or evil spirits. They believe in God; they know that God exists. They even believe in the deity of Christ. On one occasion they cried out to Jesus, "What have we to do with thee, Jesus, thou Son of God?" (Mt.8:29). But the demons are not saved. Their belief has not affected their lives and behavior at all.

Therefore, know this, know exactly what verse 20 says: "Know, O vain man, that faith without works is dead." Do not be vain (empty, useless, foolish); true faith is a living faith, a faith that works, a faith that stirs a person to live for Christ—to live righteously and purely, giving all he is and has to reach a lost and desperate world for Christ.

ILLUSTRATION:
Faith must be acted upon to be alive. Tragically, many people know the truth, but they simply are not inclined to take action. But there are those who do care. Listen to Chuck Colson's true story about a young man named Marquis and Marquis' response to the gospel message:

> *I met this young man, Marquis, in Philadelphia a couple of years ago when his grandmother came up to me after a public event and said, "Mr. Colson, thank you for sending my grandson to ... camp last summer. He was saved there— and now he's preaching the gospel to the other kids in our neighborhood."*
>
> *I talked with Marquis that day, and I was so impressed. There was a sparkle in his eye as he told me what Jesus meant to him and how he was leading others to Christ in the project in which they lived.*
>
> *His grandmother told me that ... he would have been caught up in the neighborhood gangs, doomed to follow in his father's footsteps—straight to prison. Instead, having come to faith in Christ, he was taking Jesus to the streets, sharing Christ in Camden, New Jersey, one of the toughest inner-city neighborhoods in America.*
>
> *He also worked in a church, feeding the poor—and, we've just learned this past week, talked another kid out of running away from home or maybe even suicide. He was a wonderful Christian witness to everyone he met.*
>
> *Then, two weeks ago, we received a phone call. ...Volunteers who had helped lead Marquis to Christ told us the tragic news. While walking his little brother to school, Marquis—this vibrant young evangelist—was shot and killed.*
>
> *At the funeral, our volunteers gave their condolences to Marquis's grandmother and turned to leave. But as they did, she began to shout to the hundreds of people in attendance, "You see these people? They are the reason Marquis is in heaven—they took him to camp. He met Jesus there! They are the reason I have hope!"*
>
> *Marquis's death is tragic. I don't know whether we will ever be able to control the violence, the death, and the risk in neighborhoods like this. But I do know that our hope is to take the gospel there and with it reach thousands more children. And we can pray that God will raise up more godly leaders like Marquis to help bring others to Christ. And if that happens, we will see cultural changes, one kid at a time.*[21]

Do you have a living faith, faith that takes action? True faith shares Christ with others, no matter the cost.

QUESTIONS:
1. How is real, life-changing faith different from just knowing the fact that God exists? How can you demonstrate your faith today? This week?
2. What can faith accomplish without works? Why?

5. THE MAN WHO PROVED HIS FAITH BY WORKS: ABRAHAM (vv.21-24).

There is the example of Abraham, who proved his faith by his works. Note exactly what verse 21 says:

---

[21] Charles Colson. *The Difference Faith Makes,* on BreakPoint, December 19, 2002.

"Was not Abraham our father justified by works, when he had offered Isaac his son upon the altar?" (v.21).

This is a verse that causes great problems for some people, for it seems to say that when Abraham offered up Isaac in obedience to God's instruction, he was justified. That is, Abraham was justified by works. Is a man justified by works? Is that what is meant? No! What James is saying is that Abraham *proved that he was justified by what he did—by his works*. Abraham's faith was *proven to be a true and living faith by his works*. Note what James says:

⇒ Abraham's faith wrought (brought about, worked with, cooperated with) his works (v.22). That is, his faith was acted out and proven by his works.

⇒ By his works, Abraham's faith was made perfect, that is, finished, completed, carried to the end (v.22). Abraham's faith was proven, shown to be a complete faith. A true and living faith works: it completes and finishes its course. If a faith does not work or act or complete or finish its course, it is a dead faith—an incomplete, unfinished, and unproven faith.

⇒ Abraham's faith fulfilled Scripture. What Scripture? The Scripture that said "Abraham believed God; and it was imputed unto him for righteousness" (Ge.15:6). These words were declared some thirty years before Abraham ever offered up Isaac. God pronounced that Abraham was justified and saved thirty years before this event referred to by James. James plainly declares that when Abraham offered up Isaac he was proving his faith—not earning it. The reason Abraham offered up Isaac was *because he did believe God*.

QUESTIONS:
1. Abraham offered up Isaac on an altar because he believed and trusted God. Has God ever asked you to do something difficult? What was your response? Did your response prove or disprove your faith in God?
2. On a practical level, in what ways can you increase your faith by your works?

6. THE WOMAN WHO PROVED HER FAITH BY WORKS: RAHAB (vv.25-26).

There is the example of Rahab, the converted harlot who proved her faith by works. Why mention Rahab? Because she was a harlot, the very lowest of society. She was the very opposite of Abraham, a rich and respected man. All people, even the lowest person who claims to believe in God, must do good works. They must clean up their lives and follow God. Rahab did. When the spies for Israel were being hunted down by the Jericho soldiers, she hid them. Why would she betray her country and protect the Israelite spies? Because she believed in God and His promises. She said to the spies:

"I know that the Lord hath given you the land [of promise]...for the Lord your God, he is God in heaven above, and in earth beneath" (Jos.2:9, 11).

Rahab believed in God; therefore, she acted. She put her faith to work. The conclusion is descriptive:

"For as the body without the spirit is dead, so faith without works is dead also" (v.26).

A body without the spirit or breath is dead. It does not move, act, live, or work. It is empty, totally useless and worthless. It is a dead body. So it is with faith: faith without works is dead. It does not move, act, live, or work. Faith without works is empty, totally useless and worthless. It does not live for Christ, does not follow Him in righteousness or purity nor work for Him in reaching people and meeting the needs of a destitute world.

ILLUSTRATION:
We must back up what we believe with action to demonstrate that we really believe what we say we do. We must prove our faith by our works.

The listeners stared at the speaker in disbelief. He had made a preposterous claim, saying "I have something in my pocket that no one in the world, including myself, has ever seen. And after I show it to you, no one will ever see it again." Then the man took out a peanut, cracked the shell, showed them the nut, and popped it in his mouth. —SOURCE UNKNOWN

This man backed up his words with action. Likewise, if we are to affect our world for Christ, we must show that what we claim is the truth.

QUESTIONS:
1. What promises of God inspire you to action?
2. In what ways has God asked you to put your faith into action? How did God prove Himself faithful to you when you acted in faith?
3. How has acting on your faith strengthened your commitment to the Lord?

SUMMARY:

Do you have a genuine faith? According to James, if you are not putting your faith into action, then your faith is questionable. The charge is serious: the call to action is strong. The only evidence of true faith is good works. Make up your mind today that you are going to live out your faith before others. Put yourself to the real test:
1. Ask two basic questions: (1) Can a person have faith and not do good works? (2) Can faith without works save a person?
2. Remember the professing believer who is unconcerned and neglectful.
3. Remember the two men of arrogance.
4. Remember the orthodox religionist.
5. Remember the man who proved his faith by works: Abraham.
6. Remember the woman who proved her faith by works: Rahab.

PERSONAL JOURNAL NOTES:
(Reflection and Response)

1. The most important thing that I learned from this lesson was:

2. The thing that I need to work on the most is:

3. I can apply this lesson to my life by:

4. Closing Prayer of Commitment:

CHAPTER 3

III. TEMPTATIONS & TRIALS: COMMON TO ALL, BUT ESPECIALLY TO TEACHERS, 3:1-18

A. Temptation 1: Misusining the Tongue, 3:1-12

1. The tongue—the tool of the teacher—causes the teacher to face a stricter judgment

2. The tongue stumbles & sins often

{3. The tongue is a small part of the body but it makes great boasts
   a. Two illustrations: Horses & ships

   b. The point: Control the tongue & the whole body is controlled

   c. The sin: The tongue boasts great things

4. The tongue is a

My brethren, be not many masters, knowing that we shall receive the greater condemnation. 2 For in many things we offend all. If any man offend not in word, the same is a perfect man, and able also to bridle the whole body. 3 Behold, we put bits in the horses' mouths, that they may obey us; and we turn about their whole body. 4 Behold also the ships, which though they be so great, and are driven of fierce winds, yet are they turned about with a very small helm, whithersoever the governor listeth. 5 Even so the tongue is a little member, and boasteth great things. Behold, how great a

matter a little fire kindleth! 6 And the tongue is a fire, a world of iniquity: so is the tongue among our members, that it defileth the whole body, and setteth on fire the course of nature; and it is set on fire of hell. 7 For every kind of beasts, and of birds, and of serpents, and of things in the sea, is tamed, and hath been tamed of mankind: 8 But the tongue can no man tame; it is an unruly evil, full of deadly poison. 9 Therewith bless we God, even the Father; and therewith curse we men, which are made after the similitude of God. 10 Out of the same mouth proceedeth blessing and cursing. My brethren, these things ought not so to be. 11 Doth a fountain send forth at the same place sweet water and bitter? 12 Can the fig tree, my brethren, bear olive berries? either a vine, figs? so can no fountain both yield salt water and fresh.

fire, a world of evil

a. It corrupts the whole body
b. It inflames the whole life
c. It has a source: Hell

5. The tongue is a restless evil
   a. It is the only member uncontrolled
   b. It cannot be tamed by man
   c. It is unruly, restless
      1) It is full of deadly poison
      2) It blesses God & curses man

   d. It should be controlled (by Christ)
      1) Because its behavior is inconsistent

      2) Because its behavior is contrary to our nature

Section III
TEMPTATIONS AND TRIALS: COMMON TO ALL,
BUT ESPECIALLY TO TEACHERS
James 3:1-18

STUDY 1:   TEMPTATION 1: MISUSING THE TONGUE

JAMES 3:1-12

Text: **James 3:1-12**

Aim: To determine in your heart to speak good things, not evil.

Memory Verse:

> **"Even so the tongue is a little member, and boasteth great things. Behold, how great a matter a little fire kindleth!" (James 3:5)**

INTRODUCTION:

Temptations and trials are common to all, but some are especially common to teachers. One of the greatest temptations is the abuse of the tongue. Think about the tongue for a moment. How many times have we gotten into serious trouble:

- because of an ill-spoken word?
- because of speaking without thinking?
- because of expressing our opinion in a hurtful way?
- because of some vile words we uttered?
- because we allowed a cursing to come out instead of a blessing?

James gives us some very strong advice in this lesson—advice that every believer must pay close attention to and apply. The tongue is to be used for blessing and not cursing. We must not allow our tongues to be used for evil and hellish purposes. We must put under subjection the most unruly member of our body—the untamed tongue.

OUTLINE:

1. The tongue—the tool of the teacher—causes the teacher to face a stricter judgment (v.1).
2. The tongue stumbles and sins often (v.2).
3. The tongue is a little member, boasting great things (vv.3-5).
4. The tongue is a fire, a world of iniquity (vv.5-6).
5. The tongue is a restless evil (vv.7-12).

1. THE TONGUE—THE TOOL OF THE TEACHER—CAUSES THE TEACHER TO FACE A STRICTER JUDGMENT (v.1).

Not many believers should become teachers because teachers shall face a stricter judgment from God. A teacher tells others how to live and corrects them when they come short. In fact, a teacher is responsible for the lives and spiritual growth of those under him. God holds him responsible. Therefore, if the teacher fails to live what he teaches, he will bear a greater judgment and condemnation. The teacher must live what he preaches and teaches. Note three facts.

1. This verse stresses a pointed truth: a person should commit his life to teach only if he cannot keep from teaching. Teaching is a high calling; therefore, it carries with it heavy responsibilities. Individuals failing to fulfill those responsibilities will receive the greater condemnation by God.

2. However, a person is not to fear this responsibility and neglect the gift of teaching. If he is called and gifted to teach, then he must teach. The great responsibility and potential condemnation enhances teaching's great dignity.

3. A teacher's main tool for work is speech or the tongue. Therefore, it is the tongue and its use that will have a great bearing upon a teacher's condemnation. The tongue is where the first great temptation attacks teachers, the temptation to misuse the tongue—whether to promote false or misleading information, to gain unmerited authority, to spread rumors or gossip, or simply to speak unkindly or in an arrogant manner.

QUESTIONS:
1. Has God placed the calling to teach upon your life? If so, have you heeded the call, and are you taking the role seriously?
2. In reality, we are all teachers of someone in some area of life. What responsibilities, with regard to our tongue, do we have in common with those who are *called* to teach?
3. How can an unruly tongue be a hindrance in your work for God?

2. THE TONGUE STUMBLES AND SINS OFTEN (v.2).

The tongue stumbles and sins often, stumbles in word after word. Note: "we all offend" (stumble, fall, sin). This includes teachers as well as other believers. No believer—no matter how great a teacher or who he or she is—is free from stumbling and falling. In fact, note what the verse says: "In many things" we all stumble. We do not just occasionally fall and sin; we are always coming up short before God. And this includes all teachers and preachers as well as all other believers. What is the proof of this? Our tongues. Our tongues show that we do not always love; we are not always...

- patient and longsuffering
- kind
- modest
- humble
- generous
- polite
- calm

- pure in thought, word, and deed
- rejoicing in the truth
- bearing all things
- believing God in all things
- hoping in God in all things
- enduring all things for God

In no uncertain terms, the tongue shows us that we are always stumbling and coming short. This is not to excuse us, nor to say that we are not to control the tongue. On the contrary, we are held accountable by God for every word we speak. Therefore, we must learn to control our tongues so that we can become perfect, mature, fully developed. If a person will learn to control his tongue, he can learn to control any passion or appetite of the body.

> **"In the multitude of words, there wanteth not sin: but he that refraineth his lips is wise" (Pr.10:19).**

ILLUSTRATION:

> *A fire raged on a natural gas platform that had been built out in the ocean. Firefighters worked night and day to put out the blaze, but their efforts were unsuccessful. It was discovered that the fire was so hot, it actually burned beneath the surface of the water where the pipe had been damaged and the gas was fueling the fire directly. In order to extinguish the fire, divers had to go below all the flames and cut off the gas supply first. Only then could they put out the fire above.*

How similar that blaze is to our tongue. We must go below the tongue down into the heart to cut off the ungodly emotions and evil desires that fuel the tongue. We must daily win the spiritual battle within us, the source of disagreeable talk (Js.4:1). Otherwise, the tongue will never be controlled.

QUESTIONS:
1. In what situations is it easy to offend others with your words? What do you need to do to have self-control at these times?
2. A good way to avoid speaking evil is to quote Scripture silently. What Scripture should you memorize for those times when you are tempted to misuse your tongue?

3. THE TONGUE IS A SMALL PART OF THE BODY BUT IT MAKES GREAT BOASTS (vv.3-5).

The tongue is a little member that boasts great things. Two illustrations are given.
⇒ Consider the bit or bridle that is put in the mouth of a horse to guide and turn the horse's body. The bit and bridle are very small.
⇒ Consider the rudder or helm that guides a ship. It even controls the ship through the winds of a fierce storm. Yet in proportion to the overall size of the ship, the rudder or helm is extremely small.

So it is with the tongue. It is only a little member of the body, but its destructive power is great. It can boast great things, making statements stressing our own...

- abilities
- talents
- accomplishments
- triumphs
- possessions
- position
- spirituality
- sufficiency

A person can boast about anything, and he can boast in a quiet, unassuming way or boast with many words. All boasting is destructive: either the speaker's image is lowered in the eyes of others, or the listener is made to feel inferior or less of a person than the boaster. Boasting is nothing more than vain or empty talk, but its destructive force must never be underestimated.

> "Whoso boasteth himself of a false gift is like clouds and wind without rain" (Pr.25:14).

QUESTIONS:
1. Why is boasting always destructive?
2. Compare the examples James gives of the horse and the ship to a boasting tongue.
3. What can you do to control your tongue so that you lift up others instead of boasting about yourself?

4. THE TONGUE IS A FIRE, A WORLD OF EVIL (vv.5-6).

The tongue is a fire, a world of iniquity. The word "matter" (v.5) refers to wood or a forest.[22] Therefore, the meaning of the verse is that a great forest is set on fire by only a little spark. So it is with the tongue. The tongue is a fire that can set a whole forest of lives and relationships ablaze, consuming and destroying all that lies in its path. Just think about the terrible and immense amount of damage done by the fire of words, rumors, tale-bearing, and sharp or cutting remarks. Think about the...

- marriages destroyed
- children shattered
- friendships damaged
- reputations ruined
- wars fought
- fights aroused
- injuries caused
- bodies maimed
- promotions denied

---

[22] Marvin Vincent. *Word Studies in the New Testament*, Vol.1. (Grand Rapids, MI: Eerdmans, 1969), p.747f.

The list could go on and on, but the point is well made. The tongue can be a little fire that sets ablaze and consumes a whole forest of people and relationships.

The fire of the tongue defiles the whole body and sets on fire the whole course of a man's nature or life. The phrase "the course of nature" is a descriptive phrase. It means the wheel of nature, the wheel of life, the unending span of life stretching from birth to death.[23] Therefore, the tongue can do just what this verse says: pollute and dirty a man's whole body and life. How is this possible? Think for a moment how all the evil of the world finds expression in our words...

- words that lead to immorality
- words that lead to wickedness
- words that are malicious
- words that are envious
- words that express lust
- words that curse and blaspheme
- words that express covetousness
- words that lead to idolatry
- words that lead to murder
- words that express anger
- words that are divisive

Name the sin, and words are involved either in the mind or through the tongue.

Now note the source of a fiery tongue: hell. Satan himself is the igniter of a fiery tongue; therefore, any person who sets his tongue ablaze is following the tongue of Satan, of the fire of hell itself. This person demonstrates a hellish, Satanic heart and not the heart of Christ. The fire of hell, Gehenna, is never to be seen in the life of a believer. A believer's tongue is never to speak forth the fiery flames of hell's destructive words—words that are ugly, offensive, irreverent, unclean, angry, divisive, unkind, suggestive, or sheer gossip.

> **"Whoso privily [secretly] slandereth his neighbour, him will I cut off: him that hath a high look and a proud heart will not I suffer" (Ps.101:5).**

ILLUSTRATION:

> *The story is told of a man who spent much time at a small country store catching up on and participating in town gossip. His minister simply could not convince the man of the damage he was doing. One windy day, the minister visited the man and said, "Come with me to your barn. I want to show you something." The minister had purchased a feather pillow. He said to the man, "Open this pillow and let the feathers fly out." When the man had done so, the preacher said, "Now go pick them all up."*—SOURCE UNKNOWN

The point was made. The man could no more take back all his vain talk than he could retrieve all those scattered feathers

QUESTIONS:
1. How much evil talk does it take to cause trouble and problems? Tell about a time when speaking good things avoided trouble.
2. What attitudes tempt you to speak evil? How does uplifting others help you guard against these attitudes?

5. THE TONGUE IS A RESTLESS EVIL (vv.7-12).

1. The tongue is the only creature that cannot be tamed (v.7). Men have tamed some of every kind of creature there is: beasts, birds, serpents, and creatures of the sea.

---

[23] A.T. Robertson. *Word Pictures in the New Testament,* Vol.6, p.43.

2. The tongue cannot be tamed by any man, not completely and fully. Note that verse 8 says that *no man* can tame the tongue. But God can. Matthew Henry says:

> *"No man can tame the tongue without supernatural grace and assistance."* *The apostle does not intend to represent it as a thing impossible, but as a thing extremely difficult, which therefore will require great watchfulness, and pains, and prayer.*[24]

Only Christ can control a man's tongue—control it so that it can please God.

3. The tongue is "unruly," that is, restless, uneasy, unstable, always roaming about; and it is full of deadly poison (vv.8-10). Also note how inconsistent the tongue is. It can bless God in one breath and curse men in the next. Imagine! The very same tongue that blesses is the same tongue that curses. How many sit in church on Sunday or at meals blessing God and then turn around on Monday and curse or use foul or off-colored language? It is the same tongue that does both. How restless it is! Truthfully, it is difficult to hold the tongue still; and when it speaks, it is just as liable to speak a curse word as it is to speak a blessing.

4. The tongue must be controlled by believers.
⇒ It is not fitting or right for a believer's tongue to be untamed. A believer is just like a fountain, a fountain for God. Does a fountain that is supposed to bring forth sweet water also bring forth bitter water?
⇒ It is contrary to the nature of believers to have an untamed tongue. A believer is just like a fig tree. Does the fig tree bear olives? Or a vine, figs? No fountain yields both salt and fresh water. No good tongue yields both words of blessing and words of cursing. Only an evil tongue could do this.

"A word fitly spoken is like apples of gold in picture of silver (Pr.25:11).
"Whoso keepeth his mouth and his tongue, keepeth his soul from troubles" (Pr.21:23).

QUESTIONS:
1. What happens when we try to tame our tongues on our own? What specific things do you need to do to give God control of your words?
2. In what practical ways can your words be sweet and bear fruit for the kingdom?

SUMMARY:

All of us have experienced evil at some point in life because of the tongue, both our own tongues and those of others. And we have all heard the children's lyric, "Sticks and stones may break my bones, but words can never hurt me." That may sound good as a comeback to hurtful words, but words *can* hurt; words *do* hurt. Let God help you control your tongue. Pray what King David prayed, "Let the words of my mouth, and the meditation of my heart, be acceptable in thy sight, O Lord, my strength, and my redeemer" (Ps.19:14). Do not take lightly what the tongue can do, and remember:
1. The tongue—the tool of the teacher—causes the teacher to face a stricter judgment
2. The tongue stumbles and sins often.
3. The tongue is a little member, boasting great things.
4. The tongue is a fire, a world of iniquity.
5. The tongue is a restless evil.

---

[24] Matthew Henry. *Matthew Henry's Commentary*, Vol.6. (Old Tappan, NJ: Fleming H. Revell Co., n.d.), p.985.

JAMES 3:1-12

1. The most important thing that I learned from this lesson was:

2. The thing that I need to work on the most is:

3. I can apply this lesson to my life by:

4. Closing Prayer of Commitment:

	B. Temptation 2: Misunderstanding & Twisting True Wisdom, 3:13-18	scendeth not from above, but is earthly, sensual, devilish.	God but of the earth, unspiritual & demonic
1. The wise, understanding person or teacher	13 Who is a wise man and endued with knowledge among	16 For where envying and strife is, there is confusion and every evil work.	c. Its effects: Confusion & evil
a. Shows good behavior	you? let him show out of a good conversation his works	17 But the wisdom that is from above is first pure, then peaceable, gentle, and easy	**3. The true wisdom** a. Its source: God b. Its description: Pure . . .
b. Shows humility c. Shows wisdom	with meekness of wisdom.	to be intreated, full of mercy and good fruits, without parti-	
2. The false wisdom a. Its description: Arouses envy, selfish ambition, pride, & inconsistency	14 But if ye have bitter envying and strife in your hearts, glory not, and lie not	ality, and without hypocrisy. 18 And the fruit of righteousness is sown	c. Its effects: The harvest of righteousness, peace
b. Its source: Not of	against the truth. 15 This wisdom de-	in peace of them that make peace.	

Section III
TEMPTATIONS AND TRIALS: COMMON TO ALL,
BUT ESPECIALLY TO TEACHERS
James 3:1-18

STUDY 2: TEMPTATION 2: MISUNDERSTANDING AND TWISTING TRUE WISDOM

Text: **James 3:13-18**

Aim: To understand the difference between true and false wisdom.

Memory Verse:

> **"But the wisdom that is from above is first pure, then peaceable, gentle, and easy to be intreated, full of mercy and good fruits, without partiality, and without hypocrisy" (James 3:17).**

INTRODUCTION:
What is wisdom, true wisdom? Misunderstanding wisdom is a weakness or failure on the part of all of us, but especially teachers. The leaders of this world—politicians, philosophers, preachers, and teachers—are all guilty of twisting and adjusting wisdom to mean what they want. But what is true wisdom, the kind of wisdom that brings about the good life—the kind of life and world that we should have? Is there a wisdom that can give us a world in which all men can live in peace, love, and joy and have all their needs met, even the need to conquer death and to bring about the fountain of youth? One of the greatest temptations that ever confronts teachers is the temptation to twist true wisdom.

OUTLINE:
1. The wise, understanding person or teacher (v.13).
2. The false wisdom (vv.14-16).
3. The true wisdom (vv.17-18).

JAMES 3:13-18

1. THE WISE, UNDERSTANDING PERSON OR TEACHER (v.13).

There is the wise and understanding man. Note the question, "Who is a wise man and endued with knowledge among you?" The term "wise man" refers to the teacher; *knowledge* refers to the expert, the skilled, the scientific, or knowledgeable person.[25] By teacher, of course, is meant anyone among us who teaches the Word of God, including ministers and teachers. "Do you want to be a wise teacher? Do you want to be a teacher of knowledge? Then here is how. You must do some things."

First note this: some of the teachers to whom James was writing did not understand the meaning of true wisdom and knowledge. This is the very reason for this passage: to stir ministers and teachers to think about how wise and knowledgeable they really are. A wise and knowledgeable teacher will demonstrate two traits. The words "let him show" are very emphatic. They mean that the wise teacher will strongly show forth these two traits. They will be clearly seen in his life.

1. There is the trait of good behavior and conduct. This means that the wise teacher does exactly what he should. Wisdom and knowledge have to do with how a person behaves and conducts himself, not only with knowing facts and being a scholar. A person must take the facts and apply them. This is true in any field or profession, but it is especially true in the field of Biblical teaching. A Biblical teacher must live what he teaches and preaches. He must speak words of...

- morality and purity
- righteousness and justice
- help and encouragement
- strength and edification
- ministry and challenge
- salvation and deliverance
- hope and life

But as he teaches such lessons of life, he must also live a life of *good behavior and conduct*. He must live what he teaches and preaches. He must live a moral, pure, righteous, and just life; and he must go out to minister to the needy of his community and world. The wise teacher knows that he cannot teach one thing and do another.

> "Who is wise, and he shall understand these things? prudent, and he shall know them? for the ways of the LORD are right, and the just shall walk in them: but the transgressors shall fall therein" (Hos.14:9).

2. There is the trait of meekness. The truly wise and knowledgeable teacher will show forth "meekness." The word means to be gentle, tender, humble, mild, and considerate, but strongly so. Meekness has the strength to control and discipline, and it does so at the right time.

a. Meekness has *a humble state of mind*. But this does not mean the teacher is weak, cowardly, or bowing. The meek teacher simply loves people and loves peace; he desires to be a friend to all and to help all as much as possible.

b. Meekness has *a strong state of mind*. It looks at situations and wants justice and righteousness to be done. It is not a weak mind that ignores and neglects evil and wrongdoing, abuse and suffering. Meekness actually strikes out in anger. However, note a crucial point: the anger is always at the right time and against the right thing.

---

[25] A.T. Robertson. *Word Pictures in the New Testament*, Vol.6, p.45.

c. Meekness has *strong self-control*. The meek teacher controls his spirit and mind. He dies to himself, to what his flesh would like to do, and he does the right thing—exactly what God wants done.

In summary, the meek man walks in a humble, tender, but strong state of mind; he denies himself, giving utmost consideration to others. He shows both control and righteous anger toward injustice and evil. A meek man lives for others because of what Christ has done for him.

> **"Brethren, if a man be overtaken in a fault, ye which are spiritual, restore such an one in the spirit of meekness; considering thyself, lest thou also be tempted" (Ga.6:1).**

ILLUSTRATION:

> *Evil men pursued Polycarp, a disciple of the Apostle John and a great teacher of the early Church. In those early days of Christianity, many gave their lives, being martyred for the cause of Christ. Polycarp did not resist. In fact, he even prepared a meal for those who had come to take him to his death. The proconsul insisted that Polycarp reproach Christ and say that Caesar was lord. But Polycarp replied, "Eight-six years I have served Christ, and He never once wronged me; how then shall I blaspheme my King, Who has saved me?"*[26]

What a stunning example Polycarp was! He meekly and wisely served Christ, both in word and deed, and in life and death. We also must be humble and tender, yet demonstrate a strong state of mind.

QUESTIONS:
1. What traits can be seen in a truly wise person? Which of these traits do you need to develop more?
2. Discuss why meekness is not weakness.
3. Why should you be a meek person? In what areas does pride give you the most trouble? How can you use meekness to conquer these situations?

2. THE FALSE WISDOM (vv.14-16).

There is the false wisdom and corrupt teaching of this world. This is a most tragic picture. It immediately shows us that there are teachers who follow the false wisdom of the world.
1. Note the description of false wisdom and corrupt teaching.
   a. False wisdom and corrupt teaching arouse bitter envy and jealousy. There are teachers, ministers and laymen alike, who are envious and jealous of others. In fact, false wisdom and corrupt teaching stir up a terrible division and separation between the servants of God and churches. No teacher or preacher...
   - should ever envy another person's ability, church, position, or recognition
   - should ever resent or be bitter toward former ministers or teachers
   - should ever react against being corrected because of his novel ideas for wrong behavior

---

[26] John Berry, Editor. *Foxe's Book of Martyrs*. (Grand Rapids, MI: Baker Books, 1978), p.22.

Bitterness, envy, and jealousy are all wrong. They have no place among those who teach the true wisdom of God. They are aroused by a false wisdom and a corrupt teaching.

b. False wisdom and corrupt teaching arouse a spirit of strife. The word "strife" means friction or, more accurately, selfish ambition. Unfortunately, too many of God's people—teachers and preachers included—are selfishly ambitious. Too many want...

- to be put forward, recognized, acknowledged, and honored
- to be known as wise and knowledgeable
- to be seen as *the teacher, the preacher, the leader*
- to be the builder, the creator, the founder, the originator of a new or novel idea and position or movement

In addition, there are those who seek to rally groups or parties of people around their position or belief. They are ambitious to be leaders and to have people recognize them as leaders, even if it means opposing the minister of God.

Note how restless the soul is in all of this. The soul is not at peace with itself nor with others. It is dissatisfied and ambitious for self, not for the cause of Christ or for the people of Christ. This is the way of false wisdom and corrupt teaching: it arouses strife and selfish ambition.

"Let nothing be done through strife or vainglory; but in lowliness of mind let each esteem other better than themselves. Look not every man on his own things, but every man also on the things of others" (Ph.2:3-4).

c. False wisdom and corrupt teaching arouse a spirit of boasting and self-glorying. Boasting does not necessarily mean that a person goes around boasting out loud. It refers more to what a person feels within his heart. If a person follows the way of false wisdom and false teaching, he focuses upon himself. His thoughts are upon...

- preaching a good sermon, not reaching people for Christ
- being recognized, not building up people
- securing a position, not ministering to needs

Very simply, he either seeks or feels pride in his different belief or in the position he holds. He may flaunt it publicly, making his ideas and position known, or he may just hold it silently within. In either case, his belief and position stand opposed to the wisdom and teaching of God's Word. He has allowed false wisdom and corrupt teaching to arouse a prideful and self-glorying spirit within him.

"When pride cometh, then cometh shame: but with the lowly is wisdom" (Pr.11:2).

d. False wisdom and corrupt teaching arouse a lie against the truth. This means at least two things.

⇒ First, the false teacher is inconsistent with the Word of God. He is not living and teaching the truth. He is living a lie and teaching a lie—some false doctrine, some false behavior.

⇒ Second, the false teacher is inconsistent in what he teaches and does. He teaches the truth, but he does not live the truth.

2. Note the source of false wisdom and corrupt teaching: they are not of God, but of the earth, sensual or unspiritual, and devilish.

a. False wisdom is of the earth: it centers and focuses upon the earth...

- it follows the nature of men—men of the earth—instead of God and His Word.
- it teaches the great ideas and principles of the earth instead of the ideas and principles of God and His Word.
- it challenges people to seek the goals and objectives of the earth and its leaders instead of the goals and objectives of God and His Word.
- it focuses upon life now—life upon the earth—and neglects life eternal.

The point is that heavenly wisdom, the wisdom of God and His Word (the Bible), is the basis of true wisdom. Therefore, any wisdom that neglects heavenly wisdom has a serious flaw and shortcoming. No teacher, whether minister or layman, is ever to forget this. False wisdom and corrupt teaching focus only upon the earth and neglect the wisdom from above, from God and His Word.

b. False wisdom and corrupt teaching are sensual, that is, worldly and unspiritual. They tend toward bettering man's life on earth and ignore, neglect and deny that man is spirit. They have no belief—or at most a hazy belief—in life after this world.

c. False wisdom and corrupt teaching are devilish or demonic. Such things as pride, self-ambition, bitterness, envy, strife, creating uneasiness and division, and teaching false doctrine are not of God. They are of the evil one, of the devil himself. Any teacher who selfishly seeks to promote self and does these things is following and acting just like the devil acts.

3. Note the terrible effects of false wisdom and corrupt teaching. The person who follows the false wisdom of the world—who selfishly seeks position, recognition, wealth, and authority—who seeks praise for some novel idea or doctrine he has—who disputes and clashes with others—is a false teacher who only causes confusion and every evil work. Furthermore, when that person is a minister or teacher in the church...

- he causes confusion and evil in the church: people become disturbed, divided, form cliques, and begin bearing tales. They become angry and hold feelings against one another and some even leave the church and forsake God.
- he causes confusion and evil within families: various members question, wonder, and differ with other family members. They cease to grow and many return to the world.
- he causes the weak to return to the world and to forsake God and His Word: the weak in ignorance or lack of conviction forsake Christ as the true Son of God, Christ who alone can save man.
- he causes people to attach their lives to an earthly religion of ritual, ceremony, and worldly principles—all of which die at the grave. The false teacher dooms people to an eternity apart from the Son of God, from Jesus Christ our Lord who is the Savior of the world.

The confusion and evil caused by false wisdom and corrupt teaching—by teachers who live and teach contrary to God and His Word—are endless. But this much needs to be said: the effects of corrupt teaching, of following the false wisdom of this world, should cause every minister and teacher of the church to awaken and examine their lives, beliefs, and ministries. The effects should stir many of us to repentance and confession before God.

APPLICATION:

This is a day when humility before God and His Word is needed. Why? Because there is so much false wisdom and corrupt teaching being followed. We desperately need to turn back to the worship and ministry of God alone and His Word. We need to get away from worshipping ourselves, from following our own selfish ambitions. We need to get away from seeking position, recognition, new and novel ideas, and the human comforts and ease of this life. Our call as ministers and teachers of God is to proclaim His Word and to minister to the needs of people everywhere. The confusion and evil of the world can be corrected only by proclaiming the truth of God and His Word. This we must do. And the first step is to straighten out ourselves. How? By humbly bowing before God in repentance and confession of our selfish ambition, complacency, worldliness, and lack of discipline. We must repent and confess our failure and turn completely away from it. And then we must get up and go forth in the strength of God's Spirit to proclaim the pure truth of God and His Word—proclaim His Word and nothing else.

ILLUSTRATION:

> *The devastation and debris left by the hurricane was almost unbelievable. But one house stood on its foundation. The reporter asked the owner, "Sir, why is your house the only one still standing?" "I built this house myself," the man replied. "I also built it according to the Florida state building code. When the code called for 2x6 roof trusses, I used 2x6 roof trusses. I was told that a house built according to the code could withstand a hurricane. I did, and it did. I suppose no one else around here followed the code."*

> *When the sun is shining and the skies are blue, building our lives on something other than the guidelines in God's Word can be tempting. But there is only one way to be ready for a storm.*[27] We must hold unswervingly to the Word of God; we must proclaim the truth—it and it alone.

QUESTIONS:
1. Why is false wisdom so terribly dangerous?
2. How can God's Word keep you from the trap of false wisdom?
3. What corrupt teaching has the Lord helped you to get away from?

3. THE TRUE WISDOM (vv.17-18).

There is the true wisdom of God. Note three significant points.

1. The source of true wisdom is God. True wisdom comes from above, not from this world, not from the princes and scholars of this earth. True wisdom does not come from seeking the knowledge and wisdom of men and of this world; it comes from seeking the knowledge and wisdom of God.

2. The description of true wisdom is clearly stated. The wisdom of God that is so superior to the wisdom of princes and scholars, that the ministers and teachers of God are to be teaching, is spelled out by Scripture in eight points.

    a. True wisdom is first of all *pure*. Note the word *first*. Purity is first in importance and the first thing that God gives to a man who seeks true wisdom. The one who is pure is pure from fault and defilement; it means moral purity; to be

---

[27] Edward K. Rowell, Editor. *Fresh Illustrations for Preaching and Teaching.* (Grand Rapids, MI: Copublished by Christianity Today, Inc., and Baker Books, 1997), p.147.

completely separated from impurity and wrongdoing and set apart unto God. It is not being half good and half bad, but totally pure and clean.[28] A truly wise person keeps his body pure, his relationships pure, and himself pure before God.

"Because it is written, Be ye holy; for I am holy" (1 Pe.1:16).

b. True wisdom is *peaceable*, which means to bind together; to join and weave together. It means that a wise teacher is bound, woven, and joined together...
- with God
- with his fellow man
- even with himself

The wise teacher does all he can to keep peace and to make peace where it has been broken, whether between two individuals or two groups, a family, a community, or a nation. A wise teacher, a teacher of true wisdom, works to reconcile people to God and to each other. He works to bring men closer to God and to each other.

"If it be possible, as much as lieth in you, live peaceably with all men" (Ro.12:18).

c. True wisdom is *gentle*. There is a tendency to say that either forbearance or gentleness is the better translation. It means that there is *something better than mere justice*—a gracious gentleness. The wise teacher is to be gentle and forbearing in dealing with other people.

APPLICATION:
The point is well taken: as believers, we must all be gentle and forbearing in dealing with people. The last thing we must do is criticize, condemn, censor, neglect, or ignore people. We must reach out to the world with the gospel and treat people with a *loving gentleness*. We must have absolutely nothing to do with harshness. Too many of us are harsh and critical or neglectful and withdrawn. Too many of us are wrapped in the cloak of religion, having nothing to do with reaching out to the lost. The desperate need of the hour is for all believers to reach out with the gospel in a spirit of *love and gentleness*.

"And the servant of the Lord must not strive; but be gentle unto all men, apt to teach, patient" (2 Ti.2:24).

d. True wisdom is *easy to be entreated*. This means reasonable; being willing to listen to reason and to appeal; being willing to change when one is wrong. True wisdom is not stubborn or hard. Rather, the wise teacher listens to the voice and reasoning of God and of his fellow believers; and when he is wrong, he changes his behavior.

"Come now, and let us reason together, saith the LORD: though your sins be as scarlet, they shall be as white as snow; though they be red like crimson, they shall be as wool" (Is.1:18).

---

[28] A.T. Robertson. *Word Pictures in the New Testament*, Vol.6, p.47.

e. True wisdom is *full of mercy*. The godly teacher will have feelings of pity, compassion, affection, and kindness. It is a desire to succor; to tenderly draw unto oneself and to care for. Two things are essential in order to have mercy: seeing a need, and being able to meet that need. God sees our need and feels for us (Ep.2:1-3). Therefore, He acts; He has mercy upon us. Note: mercy does not discriminate; it knows no prejudice at all. It has pity upon all, both saint and *sinner*—whoever is in need.

> **"And went to him, and bound up his wounds, pouring in oil and wine, and set him on his own beast, and brought him to an inn, and took care of him" (Lu.10:34).**

f. True wisdom is *full of good fruits*. This means that the wise teacher actually reaches out to help those in trouble. He does not experience feelings of compassion and then push them out of his mind. He acts; he meets needs; he helps the suffering, the shut-in, the prisoner, the widow and widower, the orphan, the single parent and the single-parent child, the grieving, the poor, the destitute, the homeless, the hungry, the sinner, the backslidden, the lost, and the wicked. The teacher of true wisdom reaches out with all the resources he has to reach people for Christ and to help them through all the problems and troubles of life.

> **"For I was an hungred, and ye gave me meat: I was thirsty, and ye gave me drink: I was a stranger, and ye took me in: Naked, and ye clothed me: I was sick, and ye visited me: I was in prison, and ye came unto me" (Mt.25:35-36).**

g. True wisdom is *without partiality*. The wise teacher shows no preference or favoritism to anyone. He is undivided in his convictions and judgments. He knows the truth, exactly what God's Word says, and he will not entertain false ideas or teachings. He is totally committed to following and teaching God's Word.

> **"I charge *thee* before God, and the Lord Jesus Christ, and the elect angels, that thou observe these things without preferring one before another, doing nothing by partiality" (1 Ti.5:21).**

h. True wisdom is without hypocrisy. This means to be free from insincerity, pretense, play-acting, or wearing a mask. The teacher of true wisdom does not try to deceive people; he does not teach one thing and do another thing. He does not claim to be a teacher of God's Word and then teach something other than God's Word; he does not claim to be a minister or disciple of God's Word and then live an impure and unrighteous life or an undisciplined and complacent life.

> **"In all things showing thyself a pattern of good works: in doctrine showing uncorruptness, gravity, sincerity, sound speech, that cannot be condemned; that he that is of the contrary part may be ashamed, having no evil thing to say of you" (Tit.2:7-8).**

3. The effect of true wisdom is the fruit of righteousness, a life and world of righteousness. But note how righteousness is brought about: by making peace. Righteousness—men living as they should, men treating each other and treating God as they should—can never come about unless we are at peace with each other and with God.

This means something of critical importance: *the greatest need that man has is for peace*—peace with each other and peace with God. The truly wise teacher will work continuously for peace, struggling always to get men to make peace with each other and with God. How can we ever attain such a world of peace? Only by the teachers of God—ministers and laymen alike—becoming teachers of true wisdom, teachers who make peace and who lead people to make peace with God and with each other.

QUESTIONS:
1. In terms of eternity, what has the wisdom of the world gained you?
2. Why does true wisdom come only from God?
3. What good fruit has true wisdom brought about in you? In others you know?

SUMMARY:

Unrest and dissatisfaction plague millions. People stumble around in terrible darkness, groping and grasping for peace. All the while, God is the answer—and He is the only answer. But just declaring that truth is not enough to bring peace to a person's soul. A person must gain true wisdom, which can only come from the Word of God. Therefore, the pure Word of God must be taught. People must be shown the right way to gain peace with God and with each other. Pray that the Lord will give you true wisdom so that you can live it out and share it with others. Become wise so that you can sow seeds of peace.
1. Become a wise and understanding person.
2. Recognize false wisdom.
3. Get true wisdom.

PERSONAL JOURNAL NOTES:
(Reflection and Response)

1. The most important thing that I learned from this lesson was:

2. The thing that I need to work on the most is:

3. I can apply this lesson to my life by:

4. Closing Prayer of Commitment:

	CHAPTER 4	ask not.	
	IV. TEMPTATIONS & TRIALS: TRIUMPHANTLY OVERCOME, 4:1-10	3 Ye ask, and receive not, because ye ask amiss, that ye may consume it upon your lusts.	3. Praying amiss: Praying with the wrong motive
	A. The Causes of Temptation & Wrongdoing, 4:1-6	4 Ye adulterers and adulteresses, know ye not that the friendship of the world is enmity with God? whosoever therefore will be a friend of	4. Worldliness: Friendship with the world
1. Lust, evil desires: The passion for pleasure & gratification that rages within the body	From whence come wars and fightings among you? come they not hence, even of your lusts that war in your members?	the world is the enemy of God. 5 Do ye think that the scripture saith in vain, The spirit that dwelleth in us lusteth to envy?	5. Conclusion: The cure a. Knowing that the Spirit of God yearns over you with jealousy
2. Distrust: Seeking something & never trusting God or asking God for it	2 Ye lust, and have not: ye kill, and desire to have, and cannot obtain: ye fight and war, yet ye have not, because ye	6 But he giveth more grace. Wherefore he saith, God resisteth the proud, but giveth grace unto the humble.	b. Knowing that God gives the humble believer grace & more grace, but God opposes the proud

Section IV
TEMPTATIONS AND TRIALS: TRIUMPHANTLY OVERCOME
James 4:1-10

STUDY 1: THE CAUSES OF TEMPTATION AND WRONGDOING

Text: James 4:1-6

Aim: To identify the causes of and the cure for wrongdoing.

Memory Verse:

> "But he giveth more grace. Wherefore he saith, God resisteth the proud, but giveth grace unto the humble" (James 4:6).

INTRODUCTION:

What causes temptation and wrongdoing? We are continually faced with temptations and trials, and all too often we find ourselves yielding and doing wrong. We want to do right, but often we do not. We give in. We yield to temptation, to our fleshly desires. This passage begins a new division in the book of *James,* the all-important discussion on temptations and wrongdoing, the specific target of these six verses, and how to conquer them. But before we can conquer temptations and wrongdoing, the specific target of these six verses, we must understand what causes them. Where does the rebellion within our spirits come from? Scripture gives us four causes:

JAMES 4:1-6

OUTLINE:
1. Lust, evil desires: the passion for pleasure and gratification that rages within the body and its members (v.1).
2. Distrust: seeking something and never trusting God or asking God for it (v.2).
3. Praying amiss: praying with the wrong motive (v.3).
4. Worldliness: friendship with the world (v.4).
5. Conclusion: the cure (vv.5-6).

1. LUST, EVIL DESIRES: THE PASSION FOR PLEASURE AND GRATIFICATION THAT RAGES WITHIN THE BODY (v.1).

What is the cause of temptation and wrongdoing? This Scripture says that the first cause is lust, lust warring within our bodies. What does "lust" mean? It means to crave pleasure; to crave gratification. The picture given here is that of constant warfare. Our bodies are a battlefield of wants and desires. Every person knows what it is to experience this warfare, to have his flesh yearning and yearning after something. Lust is strong and difficult to control. In fact, few people control it completely.

The point is this: man is a walking civil war; lust after lust wages war within him, seeking gratification and pleasure. Man senses one desire after another and wants to lift the restraint, to cut loose and enjoy the pleasure of the lust. It may be the lust for...

- more food
- more sex
- more money
- more property
- more recognition

Now note the result of our lust: it is fightings and wars. Remember: the greatest need that man has is for peace. Just imagine what the world would be like if men lived in peace with each other and with God. There would be no restlessness and uneasiness within the human soul and no fights and wars between men. There would be no sin or evil committed against others—wife, husband, neighbor, or anyone else—because all men would be at peace with God as well as with each other. Again, the greatest need man has is for peace. Yet, when we look at the world, what we see is anything but peace.

So, where do these fights and wars come from? What causes them? Unless we know, we can never deal with and conquer them. We must heed the Scripture: fighting comes from lust—the passion for pleasure and gratification raging within our body and its members.

A CLOSER LOOK # 1

(4:1-3) **Lust—Desire**: the word is used three times in verses 1-3. In verses 1 and 3 the word lust means out of your sinful, sensual pleasures. In verse 2 the word means a yearning passion for.[29]

Note that desire, lust, a yearning passion for is not always evil. In verse 5 the Spirit "lusts to envy." In Luke 22:15 Christ desires (yearns) to eat the Passover with the apostles. What is it that distinguishes a good desire from an evil desire? At least two major things:

1. Motive: if one desires the necessities of life, his desire is good. The necessities—food, clothing, shelter, love, care—are essential for the fullness of life. When a man seeks God for these things, God provides the necessities.

---

[29] A.T. Robertson. *Word Pictures in the New Testament*, Vol.6, p.49.

---

2. Greed: desiring food is good, but if one desires food to "consume it upon [his] lusts," that is, he desires more and more food, it is a wrong passion. It becomes sinful, sensual pleasure. Desiring love is good, but if one desires love to *consume it upon his lusts*, that is, he desires more and more love, it is a wrong passion (1 Th.4:5).

QUESTIONS:
1. Why is it so difficult to control our desires?
2. How do our desires make it difficult to have true peace within?
3. What makes a desire sinful? How does trusting God for your needs help you to avoid sinful desires?

2. DISTRUST: SEEKING SOMETHING AND NEVER TRUSTING GOD OR ASKING GOD FOR IT (v.2).

What is the cause of temptation and wrongdoing? Unbelief! Distrust! An individual does not know God in a personal way, know Him to the point that he can ask and call upon God to meet his needs. He does not have *meaningful trust* in God. He basically distrusts God.

1. The word for lust or desire in verse two is a different word than the word for lust in verses one and three. The word in this verse means a yearning desire or passion. Sometimes the desire is good; sometimes it is bad. For example, to desire food is good, but to desire excessive food is bad. This is the very point of this verse.

There is nothing wrong with our basic desires; they are to be met. But they are to be met by our trusting and depending upon God, acknowledging Him as the Source and Provider of every good and perfect gift. It is when we ignore, neglect, and deny God that our desires run loose and wild. It is when God is shoved aside that we begin to desire and crave to the point that we lie, steal, cheat, fight, kill, and go to war to gratify our desires and pleasures.

2. Second, note this: there are different levels of desires and lusts. Three levels are given in this verse.

⇒ You lust, and have not.
⇒ You desire to have and kill, and cannot obtain.
⇒ You desire to have and fight and war, yet you have not.

a. Some continually desire but they do not have. They do little to fulfill their deepest desires. They do little beyond indulging the basic desires for comfort and ease. They have broader and deeper desires, but they are just unwilling to do what is necessary to fulfill them. Most tragic of all, they do not sincerely call upon God and trust in Him to help them in meeting any of their desires, not even the desires for the basic necessities of life.
b. Some desire so much that they lie, steal, cheat, and kill to gratify and obtain their desires. The desire may be for a person, recognition, or land. But no matter what it is and no matter how much of it is gotten and possessed, it does not satisfy the lust or desire. The person simply craves more and more, not being able to obtain what he is after, even after all his sinful effort.
c. Others desire to such an extent that they are willing to fight and go to war to gratify their desires. They want something so much—some power, some land, some position, some vengeance—that they are willing to throw a whole company or nation of people into a fight or war in order to satisfy their desire and gratify their pleasure. Imagine wanting something so much that one will kill and destroy the life of another person and, in the case of war, the lives of millions in order to get it.

3. Also note this: man's deepest desires are never satisfied apart from God. A person must trust and call upon God in order to have his innermost desires fulfilled: "Ye have not, because ye ask not." There are three reasons why trusting and calling upon God are necessary for these desires to be fulfilled.

   a. Man's deepest and most restless craving is spiritual. God has made man a spiritual being, a being who is restless until his spirit is at peace with God. Man may deny, ignore, neglect, and reject this fact; nevertheless, the denial of truth does not do away with the truth. God has made man a spiritual being, a being with a soul that craves for spiritual satisfaction:

    ⇒ Man craves for God, for the fellowship and communion, the care and security of His presence.

    ⇒ Man craves for life, life that is both abundant and eternal.

    ⇒ Man craves for a perfect world.

    Man desires these things; deep down within his soul he desires spiritual satisfaction, and his spirit is restless—ever craving more and more—until the spirit is satisfied with the knowledge of these things.

   b. Man's spiritual desires and cravings cannot be satisfied with physical and material things. Man's cravings are never satisfied. They have to be controlled. If man feeds his cravings and continues to feed and feed them, he is eventually consumed by his lusts. The problem is this: man misunderstands the craving. It is an inner craving, a spiritual craving that gnaws away at him. No physical thing can satisfy that spiritual craving. Only the Spirit of God can meet the need. Throughout history men have desired everything, yet they have never been satisfied within. Why? Because what they desired was never sought from God and did not come from God.

   c. Man is not able to control his desires, not completely and not always. Man must have the presence and power of God to control all his lusts and desires. No matter what man may think and claim, history is clear evidence of the uncontrolled desires of men. In fact, any thinking and honest person can testify to his lack of control and discipline over desires and lust. We corrupt our minds, thoughts, and bodies and we hurt, disrupt, and destroy others by our uncontrolled desires and lusts. It is our uncontrolled desires and lusts that are carrying every one of us to the grave. The only escape—the only victory over the corruption of desires and lusts—is God. We must trust God and call upon God. We must consult with God about our desires and wants...

    • talk with Him

    • ask His opinion

    • ask His will

    • ask if the desire is good or bad

    • ask if the need is a true need or simply the lust for pleasure or gratification

    We must learn to commune and fellowship with God—to walk in Him, live and move in Him, seeking and asking His opinion, will, and help every step of every day. This is what God wants from all of us, leaders and citizens alike, ministers and laymen alike—God wants to fellowship and commune with us. He wants our acknowledgement—our worship and honor and praise of Him as the Lord and Father of the universe. Fellowship and communion with God—trusting and calling upon Him—is the only way we can ever fulfill the deepest and innermost desire or our hearts. And once the spiritual craving is satisfied, all of the other desires of our lives will be fulfilled and controlled by the presence and power of God in our hearts. Prayerlessness—not knowing God and not praying to God—is the second cause of temptation and wrongdoing.

"And they that are Christ's have crucified the flesh with the affections and lusts" (Ga.5:24).

ILLUSTRATION:
When we foolishly try to fulfill our desires in our own way, we are not trusting God. God is willing and certainly able to meet every need we have. But we must trust *His* plan—we must trust *Him*.

> *A man was once being [led] by a guide over a dangerous Alpine trail. At length they came to a place where a great rock jutted out over the [cliff], leaving only the fragment of a pathway. The guide laid hold on the rock with one hand and put his other hand down on what was left of the trail, the hand extending out over the abyss. He told the other man to step on his hand and forearm and thus pass around the rock in safety. The man hesitated and was afraid; but the guide said, "Do not fear to stand on my hand. That hand has never yet lost a man."*[30]

God will always provide a way out of danger or a way to escape temptation—if we will *ask* Him, and *trust* Him, and *follow* His plan.

QUESTIONS:
1. What experiences have taught you to depend upon God to meet your desires?
2. Why can we never find true and lasting fulfillment apart from God?
3. What is absolutely needed for us to control our lusts and desires?

3. PRAYING AMISS: PRAYING WITH THE WRONG MOTIVE (v.3).

What is the cause of temptation and wrongdoing? Scripture says it is praying amiss. What does it mean to pray amiss? What is a wrong prayer? Scripture tells us that we ask for things so that we can gratify our lusts and pleasure. We ask for the wrong reasons, with the wrong motives. Scripture further says that this is the reason our prayers are so often not answered. We seek God's blessings so that we can have more comfort, more enjoyment, better food and clothing, more acceptance and recognition.

What is the right motive for prayer? How can we pray and know that God will give the desires of our heart? *By asking for the glory of God.* When a person wants something from God, he must want it so that he can glorify God. We must always remember that what God is after is communion and fellowship with us, for us to draw closer and closer to Him, learning more and more about Him and worshipping and serving Him more and more. This is the way God is glorified, by our walking closely with Him and honoring and praising His name. Therefore, if we want anything from God, we must want it so that we can glorify Him—so that we can draw closer to Him and make Him better known to others.

1. If a person wants health, life, strength, or a strong testimony, it must be so that he can glorify God.

"For ye are bought with a price: therefore glorify God in your body, and in your spirit, which are God's" (1 Co.6:20).

2. If a person wants to bear fruit in his life and work, or in his church and upon his land, it must be so that he can glorify God.

---

30 Clarence E. Macartney. *Macartney's Illustrations.* (New York, NY: Abingdon Press, 1946), p. 401.

"Herein is my Father glorified, that ye bear much fruit"
(Jn.15:8).

3. If a person wants the basic necessities of life—food, clothing, and shelter, or purpose, meaning, and significance, or assurance, confidence, and security—or if he wants more position, authority, or money, it must be so that he can glorify God and the Lord Jesus Christ in his life and testimony.

"And this is the confidence that we have in him, that, if we ask any thing according to his will [glory], he heareth us: and if we know that he hear us, whatsoever we ask, we know that we have the petitions that we desired of him" (1 Jn.5:14-15).

ILLUSTRATION:

One day a lady was giving her little nephew a lesson. He was generally a good, attentive child, but on this occasion he could not fix his mind on his work. Suddenly he said, "Auntie, may I kneel down and ask God to help me to find my marble?" His aunt having given her consent, the little boy knelt by his chair, closed his eyes, and prayed silently. Then he rose and went on with his lesson contentedly. ...The next day, the lady said, "Well, dear, have you found your marble?" "No, Auntie," was the reply, "but God has made me not want to."

God does not always answer our prayers in the way we wish or expect, but if we are sincere, He will take from us the desire for what is contrary to His holy will.[31]

QUESTIONS:
1. What does it mean to pray amiss?
2. What must be the focus of all our prayers?
3. In what ways can you glorify God today?

4. WORLDLINESS: FRIENDSHIP WITH THE WORLD (v.4).

What is the cause of temptation and wrongdoing? Worldliness. James uses strong language. He calls the people adulteresses and adulterers. He means two things.
1. Being an adulteress or adulterer means that a person is guilty of spiritual adultery. Jesus Christ holds His relationship with us in the highest regard. Our relationship with Him is to be so close that it can be described only by the closeness and intimacy of marriage. In fact, our relationship with Christ can be even closer and more meaningful than marriage. We are to know, believe, and understand Christ just as we are to know, believe, and understand our husbands and wives. But with Christ there is far more of a bond and relationship than what we can have with each other as men and women on earth. Jesus Christ actually lives within our bodies in the person of the Holy Spirit. We are to live, move, and have our being in Christ and He in us. This is the reason believers are called *the bride of Christ* (2 Co.11:1-2; Ep.5:24-28; Re.19:7; 21:9).

We must never forget that our Lord gave His life and died for us. He has done everything He can to save us and to create a relationship with us. And it cost Him

---

[31] Walter B. Knight. *Knight's Master Book of 4,000 Illustrations.* (Grand Rapids, MI: Eerdmans Publishing Co., 1994), p.486.

unbelievable pain—the pain of the cross—the pain of bearing all the sins of the whole world—the pain of bearing the wrath of God against those sins—the pain of God the Father forsaking and rejecting Him when He bore our sins—pain that defies description—and it was all for us. Therefore, we must not commit spiritual adultery against Him by turning to the world. Spiritual adultery is:

⇒ not obeying the commandments of the Lord
⇒ idolatry, the worshipping of other gods
⇒ unclean works and sinful behavior
⇒ giving oneself to detestable and abominable things
⇒ forgetting God and turning one's back upon Him
⇒ refusing to turn to God and not knowing the Lord
⇒ forsaking God
⇒ disbelief in Christ
⇒ being ashamed of Christ and His Words

"How shall we escape, if we neglect so great salvation; which at the first began to be spoken by the Lord, and was confirmed unto us by them that heard him" (He.2:3).

2. Being an adulteress or adulterer means that a person is committing physical adultery. The people of James's day lived in a generation just like all other generations, a generation where immorality and all forms of sexual vices were running rampant. As Jesus said, "This is an adulterous generation"—a generation that is so full of sexual immorality that it can be characterized as adulterous. Some believers had apparently been caught up in the immorality of the world, living impure lives. They were called adulterers and adulteresses because that is just what they were. They were having affairs behind closed doors and in the dark.

3. Note a third thing, the question asked by Scripture: "Do you not know that friendship with the world is enmity with God?" What does this mean? Just what Scripture says: the person who is a friend of the world is the enemy of God. What does it mean to be a friend of the world?

⇒ It means to live for this world and the things of the world: houses, property, clothing, money, position, power, popularity, recognition, and anything else in this world that people focus upon and put before God.
⇒ It means to seek the things of this world so much that you will deceive, lie, cheat, and steal to get them.
⇒ It means to seek the fleshly pleasures and partying of this world.

Everything in this world passes away. This world is physical and material; therefore, it has the seed of corruption in it. Because of this, it stands against God. It is not eternal or holy and righteous like God. Therefore, any person who is a friend of this world also stands against God. He stands against all that God is.

QUESTIONS:
1. Why is the church, that is, believers, called "the bride of Christ"?
2. What is at the root of spiritual adultery? How can you guard against slipping away from the Lord?
3. Why is it impossible to be friends with the world and with God at the same time? In what ways can the true believer let go of the world more and more?

5. CONCLUSION: THE CURE (vv.5-6).

What is the cause of temptation and wrongdoing? This passage has told us there are four causes:

⇒ lust: the passion for pleasure and gratification
⇒ distrust: desiring something and never trusting God or asking Him for it
⇒ praying amiss: praying with the wrong motive
⇒ worldliness: friendship with the world

These are the causes of temptation and wrongdoing. Now, what is the *cure* for temptation and wrongdoing? There are two cures.

1. Believers must know this: the Spirit of God yearns over us with jealousy. Note that this point is a question: "Do you think...?" The point being made is something that we *must think about and know*. The Holy Spirit who dwells in believers...

• lusts, yearns, desires, and longs after us
• yearns with envy and jealousy over us

When does the Holy Spirit yearn over us with jealousy? All the time, but in a special way when temptation confronts us and we do wrong. The Holy Spirit is always yearning over us and He is always jealous over us. But if we turn away from Christ and become friends of the world—if we become adulterers and adulteresses—the Spirit of God does not cast us off and turn away from us. He loves us and cares for us and wants to save us. He yearns and longs for us with deep, intense jealousy—yearns and longs for us to return to Christ and to give Him our full devotion.

APPLICATION:
God has placed His Spirit into the hearts of believers to lead them through all the temptations and trials of life and to convict and lead them to repentance when they sin. The Holy Spirit yearns for and covets souls; He wants no believer to turn away from Christ.

"This I say then, Walk in the Spirit, and ye shall not fulfil the lust of the flesh. For the flesh lusteth against the Spirit, and the Spirit against the flesh: and these are contrary the one to the other: so that ye cannot do the things that ye would" (Ga.5:16-17).

2. Believers must know this: God gives the humble believer grace and more grace, but He resists the proud. Grace simply means the favor and blessings of God. When the believer faces temptation or does wrong, God meets the believer's need, no matter what it is: strength, wisdom, power, perseverance, patience, forgiveness. The believer does not deserve God's grace and blessing, but God loves him. Therefore, God gives him whatever he needs. In fact, God gives more grace, that is, an abundance of grace, overflowing grace.

But note a biblical fact: God has to stand against the sinner and his evil. God has to oppose and resist and eventually put him to the most terrible shame.

However, the glorious gospel is this: God gives grace and more grace to the humble. The person who turns to God and away from the world and his wrongdoing will receive all the grace from God he will ever need—and then some. God will look after and care for him just like a child—loving, nourishing, nurturing, feeding, clothing, sheltering, and protecting him forever and ever.

"For whosoever exalteth himself shall be abased; and he that humbleth himself shall be exalted" (Lu.14:11).

ILLUSTRATION:
God has a way of humbling the proud and blessing the humble at the same time, as is illustrated in the following humorous story:

> *An older brother always made fun of his younger siblings. The elder son prided himself in being so much smarter than his "dumb" little sister and brother. One of his favorite tricks was to make fun of them in front of his friends by offering them the choice between a nickel or a dime. He would hold out his hand with a nickel and a dime then tell them to pick which one they wanted. Each time the two little kids would go for the nickel. The young teen would then die laughing with his friends. One friend had seen the trick a dozen times so he pulled the two little kids aside and asked why they always chose the nickel. Their response was priceless. With a mischievous smile they agreed, "If we picked the dime he would quit giving us all of those nickels."[32]*

If we stay humble, we will continue to receive God's mercy. But pride will be our downfall every time.

QUESTIONS:
1. When we are tempted, what does the Holy Spirit long for us to do?
2. How does the Holy Spirit help you when you fail?
3. Why must we put aside pride in order to receive God's grace?

SUMMARY:

What do you struggle with? What cravings lie hidden within your soul? What desires want to master you? God longs, yearns to give you the grace to stand strong in the time of temptation. He will not leave your needs and desires unmet. As James says, "Submit yourselves therefore to God." This is the Good News of the Gospel: God is ever-present to forgive your sin; to meet your need; to satisfy the longing within you.

What do you need today? Our heavenly Father, the Source of every good gift, has a plentiful supply. Seek Him now. He will help you to:
1. Put aside lust and evil desires: the passion for pleasure and gratification that rages within the body and its members.
2. Put aside distrust: seeking something, and never trusting God or asking God for it.
3. Put aside praying amiss: praying with the wrong motive.
4. Put aside worldliness: friendship with the world.
5. Accept His cure for your desires.

---

32 Raymond McHenry. *McHenry's Stories for the Soul.* (Peabody, MA: Hendrickson Publishers, 2001), #1537.

JAMES 4:1-6

PERSONAL JOURNAL NOTES:
(Reflection and Response)

1. The most important thing that I learned from this lesson was:

2. The thing that I need to work on the most is:

3. I can apply this lesson to my life by:

4. Closing Prayer of Commitment:

	B. The Way to Overcome Temptation, 4:7-10	ye sinners; and purify your hearts, ye double minded.	b. Must have a pure heart
1. Step 1: Submit to God—resist the devil	7 Submit yourselves therefore to God. Resist the devil, and he will flee from you.	9 Be afflicted, and mourn, and weep: let your laughter be turned to mourning, and your joy to heaviness.	3. Step 3: Be disciplined & deeply or mournfully concerned
2. Step 2: Draw near to God & repent a. Must have clean hands	8 Draw nigh to God, and he will draw nigh to you. Cleanse your hands,	10 Humble yourselves in the sight of the Lord, and he shall lift you up.	4. Step 4: Humble yourself

Section IV
TEMPTATIONS AND TRIALS: TRIUMPHANTLY OVERCOME
James 4:1-10

STUDY 2:   THE WAY TO OVERCOME TEMPTATION

Text: James 4:7-10

Aim: To learn the Biblical steps to withstanding temptation.

Memory Verse:

"**Submit yourselves therefore to God. Resist the devil, and he will flee from you**" (James 4:10).

INTRODUCTION:
Temptation is the constant experience of man. Temptation comes, and then comes sin. Every sin is preceded by temptation. Therefore, if we can figure out how to overcome temptation, we can wipe sin off the face of the earth. Imagine a world without sin—without war, murder, assault, divorce, immorality, hatred, anger, arrogance, haughtiness, and neglect. On and on the list could go. Imagine an existence where all sin was eradicated. Again, the answer to conquering sin is to conquer temptation. Deal with the cause, not the result. How can we overcome and conquer temptation? This is the discussion of this passage. We must do four things.

OUTLINE:
1. Step 1: submit to God—resist the devil (v.7).
2. Step 2: draw near to God and repent (v.8).
3. Step 3: be disciplined and deeply or mournfully concerned (v.9).
4. Step 4: humble yourself (v.10).

1. STEP ONE: SUBMIT TO GOD—RESIST THE DEVIL (v.7).

How can we overcome temptation? By submitting to God, obeying His every word.
⇒ To "submit" to God means to put yourself under God, under His care, power, and strength; to yield to God, to His will, command, instructions, laws, behavior, and Word; to surrender yourself to God for Him to strengthen you so that you can do exactly what He says.

⇒ To "resist" here means to take a stand against the devil; to exert the energy and effort to oppose and defeat the devil and his temptation; to keep your mind and energy focused upon counteracting and conquering the temptation of the devil.

Both of these words are military words; therefore, they are urgent and they are imperatives. They are from our military commander, God Himself. When temptation strikes, submit yourself to God. Do exactly what your military commander says. He has the overall plan and all the weapons and firepower at His disposal. His grace and power can defeat the enemy.

Submit yourself to God and His Word of command. What this means is to focus your mind upon God and His Word *immediately when temptation strikes*. Turn away from the temptation, push it out of your mind and begin to think about God and go over and over His Word in your mind. Persevere in following God's command and in resisting the devil. When you do, the most wonderful thing will happen. The devil will flee and the temptation will be gone. Remember: this is exactly what Christ did (see Lu.4:4, 8, 12).

Now, note the critical point: we must both surrender to God and *resist the devil*. Both acts are required. When the devil or temptation confronts us, we can never defeat him and his hoards of evil...

- by standing and fighting alone
- by going our own way
- by giving in a little
- by refusing to listen to our Commander's Word.

We cannot even listen to the enemy's tempting offer—not even for a moment. Picturing the temptation moves us a long way down the road toward defecting, moving into the enemy's camp, and sinning against God. The only way to conquer temptation is to *immediately* submit ourselves to God and *immediately* resist the devil and his temptation. (See A CLOSER LOOK #1 below.)

A CLOSER LOOK # 1

(4:7) Satan—Temptation—Believer, Victory: the believer is to resist the devil. He is to overcome the *evil one*. But how?

⇒ By asking God and praying, "Deliver us from the evil one."

> **"And lead us not into temptation, but deliver us from evil: for thine is the kingdom, and the power, and the glory, for ever" (Mt.6:13).**

⇒ By quoting Scripture, fasting and praying.

> **"And when the tempter came to him, he said, If thou be the Son of God, command that these stones be made bread. But he answered and said, It is written, Man shall not live by bread alone, but by every word that proceedeth out of the mouth of God" (Mt.4:3-4).**

⇒ By ministering in Jesus' name.

> **"And the seventy returned again with joy, saying, Lord, even the devils are subject unto us through thy name" (Lu.10:17).**

⇒ By special sessions of prayer.

> **"And the Lord said, Simon, Simon, behold, Satan hath desired to have you, that he may sift you as wheat: but I have**

prayed for thee, that thy faith fail not: and when thou art converted, strengthen thy brethren" (Lu.22:31-32).

$\Rightarrow$ By invoking, that is, claiming, the name and power of the God of peace.

"And the God of peace shall bruise Satan under your feet
shortly" (Ro.16:20).

$\Rightarrow$ By forgiving others.

"To whom ye forgive any thing, I forgive also: for if I forgave
any thing, to whom I forgave it, for your sakes forgave I it in the
person of Christ; lest Satan should get an advantage of us: for we
are not ignorant of his devices" (2 Co.2:10-11).

$\Rightarrow$ By not giving place to the devil, that is, not allowing the devil to get a foot-
hold, not get a foot in the door, not get a chance to further tempt you.

"Neither give place to the devil" (Ep.4:27).

$\Rightarrow$ By putting on the whole armor of God.

"Finally, my brethren, be strong in the Lord, and in the
power of his might. Put on the whole armour of God, that ye may
be able to stand against the wiles of the devil" (Ep.6:10-11; see
vv.12-18).

$\Rightarrow$ By repenting and acknowledging the truth.

"In meekness instructing those that oppose themselves; if God
peradventure will give them repentance to the acknowledging of
the truth; and that they may recover themselves out of the snare
of the devil, who are taken captive by him at his will" (2 Ti.2:25-
26; Ac.13:10).

$\Rightarrow$ By resisting the devil.

"Submit yourselves therefore to God. Resist the devil, and he
will flee from you" (Js.4:7; 1 Pe.5:8-9).

$\Rightarrow$ By being born again.

"We know that whosoever is born of God sinneth not; but he
that is begotten of God keepeth himself, and that wicked one
toucheth him not" (1 Jn.5:18).

$\Rightarrow$ By not fearing and by being faithful.

"Fear none of those things which thou shalt suffer: behold,
the devil shall cast some of you into prison, that ye may be
tried; and ye shall have tribulation ten days: be thou faithful
unto death, and I will give thee a crown of life. He that hath
an ear, let him hear what the Spirit saith unto the churches;
He that overcometh shall not be hurt of the second death"
(Re.2:10-11).

ILLUSTRATION:

> The sign read, "WARNING! DANGER! Stay on the high bank." But a man passing by did not heed the sign. He had seen something of interest beside the stream—an old log of unusual structure lying there in the reeds. The man was a wood-carver and thought, "This will make a spectacular piece to work with." He climbed down the steep ground to the water below, being very careful at first. But the closer he got to the log, the more excited he became. Then, the "log" moved. The man tried to bolt, but the mother crocodile, protecting her eggs, was much faster and stronger. The man had no chance of making it back to the safe high path.

What if the man had heeded the sign when he was first tempted to go down by the river? How much trouble and destruction would have been avoided? Likewise, if we simply heeded God's instructions, yielding to His Holy Word as soon as we were tempted, how much trouble and destruction would we avoid?

QUESTIONS:
1. On a day-to-day basis, how can you to submit to God and resist the devil?
2. What example did Jesus Christ give us for battling temptation?
3. Name several weapons available to you to resist the devil.

2. STEP TWO: DRAW NEAR TO GOD AND REPENT (v.8).

How can we overcome temptation? The second thing we must do to overcome temptation is to draw near God, repenting of our sins. This is the greatest privilege in all the world: to have the glorious privilege to approach and draw near God, the Sovereign Majesty of the universe, the Creator and Lord of the universe. Just think, believers can approach God and talk and share with Him anytime, anyplace. The door into God's presence is never closed. But note what Scripture teaches: the door into God's presence is not only open, but we are *strongly urged and encouraged* to draw near God. This verse is again a strong imperative: "Draw near to God." The temptation strikes; it is immediate, unexpected, fierce. What can we do? What is our hope? God—draw near to God. The idea is more than just submitting to God, much more. *Drawing near* means to get as close as possible to God. Get right next to Him. Begin to talk and share with Him. How do we do this?
   ⇒ By reading the Word of God, the Holy Bible or, if we do not have access to God's Word when the temptation strikes, by reviewing verses of Scripture over and over in our minds.
   ⇒ By prayer—by asking God for strength and power, mercy and grace. But note: the prayer should be positive, focusing upon God and His strength and Word, not upon the temptation. Keep your mind off the temptation and upon God.

Focus upon God and God alone. Get close to God. Draw as near as possible to Him and note the glorious promise: God will draw near you. He will draw near and embrace you and strengthen you and deliver you. This is exactly what God promises.

However, note that drawing near to God is conditional. There is a person who God does not allow to draw near Him. Who? The person with unclean, sinful hands and an impure, wavering heart. A person must do two things before he can draw near God.

1. The person must clean his hands. Some of the Christians James was writing to had unclean, sinful hands, and James called them just what they were: *sinners*. If any of us have unclean hands—if we have touched what God forbids us to touch—we have

not only sinned, but we are *sinners*. A terrible title to have attached to our names! Nevertheless, Scripture says that a person who touches when God says not to touch is a *sinner*.

The point is this: our hands must be cleansed of sin before we can approach and draw near God. God will not respond—He will not draw near—to a person whose hands are not cleansed of sin.

2. The person must purify his heart and quit wavering between God and temptation. A person cannot have a divided loyalty between God and the world. A person who is double-minded, who tries to follow God some of the time and the world at other times, cannot draw near God. God does not accept him nor draw near him. A person must purify his heart, turn his heart completely and totally over to the Lord Jesus Christ. A pure heart—a heart totally committed and loyal to Jesus Christ—is the only heart that God will accept and draw near.

ILLUSTRATION:

Drawing near to God means pulling away from temptation. But we must look to God to deliver us from the sinful desire that threatens to take control of us. In other words, we must desire God more than we desire the world.

> *A young Christian was invited to a party one weekend. He knew the planned events were anything but wholesome and godly, but he really wanted to be part of the in-crowd. However, he could not get away from the gnawing conviction in his heart. All week, he wavered between forbidden thoughts of upcoming affair and waves of guilt for even considering going to the party.*
>
> *Finally, the young man hit upon a plan. He would ask his father for permission to go. Of course, he would be careful not to reveal the details of the event. If his father gave him permission, all would be well—or so he thought. When Friday came, he went to his father and carefully asked for his okay, choosing each word with considerable thought.*
>
> *After patiently listening, the boy's father replied, "I have only one question." "What's that?" the youth asked, still confident in his plan. "If the Lord comes back tonight," his father continued, "do you want Him to find you at that event?" After thanking his father the young man meekly walked away and forgot about his plans for the party.*

God is always present to deliver us from trouble, but He would much rather deliver us from the *temptation* to get into trouble.

QUESTIONS:

1. What two ways should we use to draw close to God every day?
2. What conditions must be met in order to draw near to God?
3. What are some specific ways you can battle temptation?

3. STEP THREE: BE DISCIPLINED AND DEEPLY OR MOURNFULLY CONCERNED (v.9).

How can we overcome temptation? We must consider the temptation to be serious, very serious. Note how descriptive this verse is:

> **"Be afflicted, and mourn, and weep: let your laughter be turned to mourning, and your joy to heaviness" (v.9).**

The word for "be afflicted" means to endure toils;[33] to discipline and to voluntarily abstain.[34] Temptation is affliction; therefore, when tempted, it is time to be disciplined and to control the comforts and joys of life. Temptation is a time for rigorous warfare—for battle and the discipline and endurance of battle.

In fact, note this: the strife of temptation is usually immediate and unexpected. Therefore, we must immediately drop whatever we are doing—immediately stop the laughter and the comforts or joy of the moment—and focus upon getting near God. Our hearts must mourn and weep under the heaviness of the temptation and its attack, mourn and weep before God, asking for strength and deliverance, lest we disappoint and cut the heart of Christ.

When we take the temptation this seriously, God will hear our cry and deliver and save us.

> **QUESTIONS:**
> 1. What should be our attitude toward temptation? How can you become more sensitive to your own particular temptations?
> 2. What should be our first reaction when temptation strikes?
> 3. How has God helped you in the past to conquer temptation? What steps did you take to receive His help?

4. STEP FOUR: HUMBLE YOURSELVES IN THE SIGHT OF THE LORD (v. 10).

How can we overcome temptation? God sees us at all times, even when we are tempted. Therefore, when we are tempted...

- God must not see us continuing on in our activity and comfort, laughter and joy of the moment. God must see us drawing near Him and mourning and crying for deliverance.

- God must not see a self-sufficient spirit, a spirit that overlooks calling upon Him. God must not see a spirit that ignores His Word, a spirit that faces the temptation on its own, ignoring and not even thinking about God and His Word and strength. God must see us humbly coming into His presence, calling and depending upon Him for strength and wisdom to overcome the temptation.

- God must not see us looking at the temptation and picturing how attractive and enticing it is. He must not see us reveling in the thoughts of the temptation and in picturing how nice it would be. God must see us "casting down every imagination and bringing into captivity *every thought* to the obedience of Christ" (2 Co.10:5). Imagine! Every thought is to be captured and made obedient to Christ. We must always remember that the spiritual warfare is fought in the spirit and mind, at the very core of the heart and mind. We must commit our hearts and minds to *focus totally* upon Christ and things that are true, honest, just, pure, lovely, of good report, virtuous, and praiseworthy (Ph.4:8). This unbroken communion and fellowship with Christ is what God is after. It is the very reason He created us and has now saved us.

The point is this: when a person is tempted, if he will humble himself in the sight of God, God will lift him up. God will meet his need, give him whatever he needs, and deliver him from the onslaught of temptation.

---

[33] A.T. Robertson. *Word Pictures in the New Testament*, Vol.6, p.53.
[34] William Barclay. *The Letters of James and Peter*, p.127.

APPLICATION:
William Barclay has an excellent description of this point.

> *Only when a man realizes his own ignorance can he ask the guidance of God. Only when a man realizes his own poverty in the things that matter will he pray for the riches of God's grace. Only when a man realizes his weakness in necessary things will he come to draw upon his strength of God. Only when a man realizes that he cannot cope with life by himself will he kneel before the Lord of all good life. Only when a man realizes his own sin will he realize his need of a Saviour and of the forgiveness of God.*[35]

"Though the LORD be high, yet hath he respect unto the lowly: but the proud he knoweth afar off" (Ps.138:6).

QUESTIONS:
1. What does God want and expect us to do when temptation comes?
2. Since spiritual battles are fought in the mind, what is our best defense for avoiding temptation in the first place?
3. Read Ph. 4:8. What good, pure, and lovely things can you think about during temptation?

SUMMARY:

Remember what James 4:6 says: God resists the proud but gives grace to the humble. Without God's grace, we cannot stand during temptation. We will crumble under the weight or pressure of the overwhelming desire or enticement. Therefore, submitting to God is the only way to escape the traps and destruction of the devil. When we submit and draw near to the Lord, we will experience a close, precious fellowship with Him, and He will enable us to conquer and avoid temptation.
1. Step 1: submit to God—resist the devil.
2. Step 2: draw near to God and repent.
3. Step 3: be disciplined and deeply or mournfully concerned.
4. Step 4: humble yourself.

PERSONAL JOURNAL NOTES:
(Reflection and Response)

1. The most important thing that I learned from this lesson was:

2. The thing that I need to work on the most is:

3. I can apply this lesson to my life by:

4. Closing Prayer of Commitment:

---

[35] William Barclay. *The Letters of James and Peter*, p.129.

	V. TEMPTATIONS & TRIALS: COMMON TO ALL, BUT ESPECIALLY TO THE GIFTED, 4:11–5:6	of his brother, and judgeth his brother, speaketh evil of the law, and judgeth the law:	**2. Judging others violates the law of God**
	A. Temptation 1: The Judge—Judging Others, 4:11-12	but if thou judge the law, thou art not a doer of the law, but a judge.	**3. Judging others sets one up as judge, as a lawgiver**
1. Judging others is slander, speaking evil of brothers	11 Speak not evil one of another, brethren. He that speaketh evil	12 There is one lawgiver, who is able to save and to destroy: who art thou that judgest another?	**4. Judging others usurps God's right & authority**

Section V
TEMPTATIONS AND TRIALS: COMMON TO ALL, BUT ESPECIALLY TO THE GIFTED
James 4:11–5:6

STUDY 1: TEMPTATION 1: THE JUDGE—JUDGING OTHERS

Text: **James 4:11-12**

Aim: To understand and avoid the evil of criticism.

Memory Verse:

"Speak not evil one of another, brethren" (James 4:11).

INTRODUCTION:

God hates all sin, but there are a few sins that are constantly and strongly condemned by Scripture. Judging others—criticizing, backbiting, gossiping, speaking evil, and talking about others—is one of the sins that Scripture consistently and severely condemns.

Temptations and trials commonly confront all of us, but some are especially common to the gifted. And note what the first temptation is that confronts the person who is especially gifted: judging others. Condemning or criticizing others is one of the most evil of all sins, a sin of terrible pride. Why? Simply this: the person who judges and condemns another person is committing the original sin—the foolish sin of trying to take the very place of God. God will never allow such a sin. Pride will always be met with swift judgment. Note four unmistakable facts about judging others.

OUTLINE:

1. Judging others is slander, speaking evil of brothers (v.11).
2. Judging others violates the law of God (v.11).
3. Judging others sets one up as judge, as a law-giver (v.11).
4. Judging others usurps God's right and authority (v.12).

1. JUDGING OTHERS IS SLANDER, SPEAKING EVIL OF BROTHERS (v.11).

Note three significant points.

1. "Speaking evil" means to criticize, judge, condemn another person. It means to tear down another person; to lower his image and reputation in the eyes of others. The word usually means to talk about a person behind his back, when he is not present.

2. Note that a brother has sinned. He has broken the law of God. He has failed, and his failure is known. It is public knowledge, and he is being judged and criticized for his failure. He is being talked about. Now, if we are forbidden to speak evil of a person who is actually guilty of sin, how much more are we forbidden to speak against a person just because we dislike or disagree with him?

Note what the Scripture says: this is *evil speaking*. It is just as much an evil as the failure of the other person. Therefore, the person who judges another is as guilty as the sinner.

3. The exhortation is strong: Christian believers are not to judge or speak evil of one another. The reason is clear: we are brothers, brothers of Christ and of one another. All of us are of the family of God. Therefore, we are to love, support, and build up one another, and not tear down one another.

When we criticize a brother or sister in Christ, we are slandering one of God's own children, slandering a son or daughter of God. This alone should keep us from speaking evil of our brothers in Christ.

Think about something else as well: there is never a spirit of evil speaking in the truly humble and loving person. There is only a loving compassion for others, especially for those who have come short and fallen. Therefore, when we speak evil of another person, it means that we are neither humble nor loving, but the very opposite: prideful and hateful. We are evil speakers.

ILLUSTRATION:

> *The great evangelist, John Wesley, knew what damage evil speaking could do, both to the work of the Kingdom and to his ministers. The following was found in the handwriting of John Wesley after his death and was signed by him, his brother Charles, and several other fellow ministers in the Methodist revival.*
>
> *"It is agreed by us whose names are underwritten:*
> 1. *That we will not listen to or willingly inquire after any ill concerning each other.*
> 2. *That if we do hear any ill of each other, we will not be forward to believe it.*
> 3. *That as soon as possible we will communicate what we hear by speaking or writing to the person concerned.*
> 4. *That till we have done this we will not write or speak a syllable of it to any other person whatever.*
> 5. *That neither will we mention it after we have done this, to any other person.*
> 6. *That we will not make any exception to any of these rules unless we think ourselves absolutely obliged in conscience so to do."*
> —From the personal writings of John Wesley—SOURCE UNKNOWN

Did John Wesley go too far? Was he too serious? Not according to the Bible. "And who are we to argue with the Bible?"

QUESTIONS:
1. How is judging others rebellion against God?
2. Consider Wesley's rules about gossip. What rules do you follow already? Which of these do you need to adopt?
3. How does humility keep you from speaking evil?

2. JUDGING OTHERS VIOLATES THE LAW OF GOD (v.11).

Note exactly what Scripture says:

> **"He that speaketh evil of his brother, and judgeth his brother, speaketh evil of the law" (v.11).**

This is a shocking statement: talking about and slandering a brother is speaking evil of the law. What does this mean? When a person talks about and condemns others, he is violating the greatest of all laws, the royal law of love, the law that plainly declares that we are to love our neighbors as ourselves (Js.2:8). The criticizer and backbiter himself becomes guilty of transgression, and his transgression violates the great law that commands us to love one another. In fact, the criticizer and backbiter does more harm than the person he is judging. The criticizer and backbiter is speaking evil of the law; that is, he is condemning another person for some failure while he himself is breaking the law. He is saying that the law of love is not all that important, that it can sometimes be ignored, neglected, abused, or violated. The person who talks about others is a double hypocrite: he not only ignores the great law of love by talking about others, but he also slanders others for their failure. He is, as Scripture says, speaking evil of the law. His speaking evil against his brother does not uphold the law of love; it speaks evil and tears down the law of love.

> **"For all the law is fulfilled in one word, even in this; Thou shalt love thy neighbour as thyself" (Ga.5:14).**
> **"If ye fulfil the royal law according to the Scripture, Thou shalt love thy neighbour as thyself, ye do well" (Js.2:8).**

QUESTIONS:
1. What is the "royal law of love"? How can you keep this law when there are people you strongly disagree with or disapprove of?
2. What does criticism reveal about the person criticizing others? What steps can *you* take to be less critical?

3. JUDGING OTHERS SETS ONE UP AS A JUDGE OR AS A LAWGIVER (v.11).

Again, note exactly what the Scripture says:

> **"He that speaketh evil of his brother, and judgeth his brother... judgeth the law" (v.11).**

How is this possible? How do criticizing and backbiting and judging a brother make us judges of the law? When we criticize a brother, we are saying that the law he has broken is important, very important—so important that he should not have broken it— but the law of love is not important enough to keep us from criticizing him. We judge the law he has broken as important and the law of love as not so important. Note: this is a very common practice. We choose which laws should be kept and which can be occasionally broken. It may be the laws governing gluttony, anger, worship, sex, what we look at and desire, drunkenness, covetousness, or the great law of love being discussed in this passage. But no matter what the law is, we judge the law when we *choose...*

- which laws are important and which laws are not so important
- which laws are binding and which laws are not so binding
- which laws deserve our utmost attention and which laws do not deserve so much attention
- which laws should be kept and which laws can occasionally be broken

When we choose what laws we will obey, we set ourselves up above the law of God. We make ourselves the judge of the law; we make ourselves lawgivers. And note: this is not our function. Scripture declares plainly that our duty is to obey the law, not to be judges of the law. This is exactly what the end of verse 11 says: "If you judge the law, you are not a doer of the law, but a judge." We are not to criticize our brother or sister. Contrariwise, we are to do the very thing our brother or sister is to do: keep the law of God.

> **"And thinkest thou this, O man, that judgest them which do such things, and doest the same, that thou shalt escape the judgement of God" (Ro.2:3).**
> **"For not the hearers of the law are just before God, but the doers of the law shall be justified" (Ro.2:13).**

ILLUSTRATION:
We are all guilty under the Law and need God's mercy. But having received mercy does not qualify us as judges. We must stay humble, realizing that we are in continual need of God's grace, as the following poem so well states:

WHEN I SAY I AM A CHRISTIAN

When I say ... "I am a Christian"
I'm not shouting, "I am saved."
I'm whispering, "I was lost!"
That is why I chose this way.

When I say ... "I am a Christian"
I don't speak of this with pride.
I'm confessing that I stumble
and need someone to be my guide.

...When I say ... "I am a Christian"
I'm not bragging of success.
I'm admitting I have failed
and cannot ever pay the debt.

...When I say ... "I am a Christian"
I do not wish to judge.
I have no authority.
I only know I'm loved.
                    —AUTHOR UNKNOWN[36]

---

36 Ken Krivolahvek. *Rejoicin' an' Repentin'*. (Olathe, KS: KLK Ministries, 2002), p. 118.

QUESTIONS:
1.   Why is judging another person a sin against God? What is your attitude supposed to be if you see someone break a law?
2.   How can being thankful for your salvation keep you from being critical?

4. JUDGING OTHERS USURPS GOD'S RIGHT AND AUTHORITY (v.12).

This verse is clear and forceful; it is a very strong warning to the criticizer and backbiter.

"There is one lawgiver, who is able to save and to destroy: who art thou that judgest another?" (v.12).

God alone is the great Lawgiver, and Scripture declares: "There is [only] *one* lawgiver." He and He alone has given the laws that are to judge and condemn our neighbors. Note closely: when we judge, criticize, and backbite our brothers, we are usurping God's right to judge men. We are setting ourselves up in the place of God, making ourselves God—claiming the right to sit in judgment upon our brother. No person, not one of us, has the right to sit upon the throne of God's judgment. Judgment and condemnation—criticizing, talking about, and picking out the shortcomings and failures of any brother—are God's right and His alone. No one has the right to judge but God Himself.

This is very strong language. God is not going to tolerate a person setting himself up as the judge, as God Himself, over someone else—not when the one who sits in judgment is but a mere sinful man who is ever so short himself.

Note one other fact as well: judging, condemning, criticizing, and talking about a person destroys the person. This is exactly what this verse says. There is only one Person who is *able to save and destroy*—only one Person who can judge and criticize another person as being either good or bad, as either worthy of being saved or destroyed—and that Person is God. God and God alone can save and destroy, not man. Not one of us is able to know and judge the whole truth about a person. Therefore, "who are you that you judge another person"—who do you think you are? God?

APPLICATION:
There are several reasons why we should never criticize another person.
1) All the circumstances and all the facts are never known. What happened and why it happened are not fully known. And unfortunately there is something seldom remembered: when people emerge from the closed doors and enter the public, the one who does the talking does not always reveal the true facts. The spirit of talking to others is the spirit of self-justification. The spirit of silence is the spirit of caring and compassion, which desires no hurt for others.
2) All people—religious as well as non-religious—come short, fail, and fall. And we all sin often (1 Jn.1:8, 10). No one is ever exempt from sin. When we criticize and judge, we have a problem: we forget that we are sinners. When we acknowledge our own true condition, we act with care and compassion toward all who come short. The believer must always remember that his righteousness is Jesus Christ, and he is *always* dependent upon Christ's righteousness (2 Co.5:21; Ph.3:8-16).
3) All there is to know about a person is never known. How, then, can we criticize? Think about childhood for a moment. So much goes into influencing a human life that only God can know a person, know him well enough to judge him. Certainly we can never know one another well enough to pass judgment.

4) Judging others usurps God's authority. When a person criticizes another, he is saying that he is worthy and has the right to be *the judge* over other lives. He is claiming the right to be God, which is ridiculous.

"Judge not, that ye be not judged" (Mt.7:1).

QUESTIONS:
1. Why is judging others such a prideful sin?
2. When tempted to criticize someone, what can you do to prevent yourself from speaking—or even thinking—the judgmental words?

SUMMARY:

A few critical words, an air of superiority, a look of rejection—all of these can cut a brother or sister ever so deeply. Judging and criticizing others is a terrible evil. As believers, we must take great care to avoid condemning one another. The work of Christ, of His church, cannot move forward in an atmosphere of criticism and disapproval. For this reason, we must not attack or pass judgment on others. We are to work alongside one another in unity. James strongly warns us to repent of our critical attitudes and to always remember:
1. Judging others is speaking evil of brothers.
2. Judging others violates the law of God.
3. Judging others sets one up as judge, as a law-giver.
4. Judging others usurps God's right and authority.

PERSONAL JOURNAL NOTES:
(Reflection and Response)

1. The most important thing that I learned from this lesson was:

2. The thing that I need to work on the most is:

3. I can apply this lesson to my life by:

4. Closing Prayer of Commitment:

	B.Temptation 2: The Humanist— Boasting Self- Sufficiency, 4:13-17	is your life? It is even a vapour, that appeareth for a little time, and then vanisheth away.	**life**
1. Self-sufficiency is planning without God	13 Go to now, ye that say, To day or to morrow we will go into such a city, and continue there a year, and buy and sell, and get gain:	15 For that ye ought to say, If the Lord will, we shall live, and do this, or that. 16 But now ye rejoice in your boastings: all such rejoicing is evil.	**3. Self-sufficiency is failure to acknowledge God**
2. Self-sufficiency is failure to recognize the uncertainty of	14 Whereas ye know not what shall be on the morrow. For what	17 Therefore to him that knoweth to do good, and doeth it not, to him it is sin.	**4. Self-sufficiency is boasting, bragging, & showing arrogance** **5. Self-sufficiency is sin**

Section V
TEMPTATIONS AND TRIALS: COMMON TO ALL BUT ESPECIALLY TO THE GIFTED
James 4:11–5:6

STUDY 2:   TEMPTATION 2: THE HUMANIST—BOASTING SELF-SUFFICIENCY

Text: **James 4:13-17**

Aim: To lean more on God, less on self, for direction in your life.

Memory Verse:

"For that ye ought to say, If the Lord will, we shall live, and do this, or that" (James 4:15).

INTRODUCTION:
Self-sufficiency is a terrible sin in the eyes of God. The reason is because man is ever so frail, infirmed, corruptible, and subject to disease, accidents, and death at the snap of a finger. Yet despite his frailty and the uncertainty of his life, man still ignores God and walks upon earth as though his future is totally in his own hands. This is the whole philosophy of humanism, the boast that man is the ultimate being in control of his life and fate. Such a boast is utter foolishness when man is nothing more than a speck compared to God, our all-knowing and all-powerful Creator. Humanism or self-sufficiency is so unreasonable and illogical that it is totally unworthy of a thinking and honest being. Yet it is the very position and philosophy, the very lifestyle chosen by so many people. This is the subject of the present passage: the terrible sin of humanism, of boasting self-sufficiency, the temptation that strikes so many of the gifted people of this earth.

OUTLINE:
1. Self-sufficiency is planning without God (v.13).
2. Self-sufficiency is failure to recognize the uncertainty of life (v.14).
3. Self-sufficiency is failure to acknowledge God (v.15).
4. Self-sufficiency is boasting, bragging, and showing arrogance (v.16).
5. Self-sufficiency is sin (v.17).

1. SELF-SUFFICIENCY IS PLANNING WITHOUT GOD (v.13).

There is nothing wrong with making plans. We should plan and prepare for the future. In fact, we should never fail to take the time to plan. Scripture is very clear about this: we are not to be slothful in business or in any endeavor (Ro.12:11). But planning before we act is not what this Scripture is talking about; it is warning us *not to plan without God*.

Yet despite warning after warning in Scripture, most people plan their lives without God. They plan as if their own will and desire controls the destiny of life. Note the example of Scripture (v.13): How many plan to do this or that, whether small plans or great plans, yet in all their planning do not consider God—not to the point of making sure that it is His will they are doing? Not making sure that they acknowledge Him in all their ways? Why does man not acknowledge God as he lays plans and then carries out his plans? Because of self-sufficiency. Frankly, most people feel little need for God. They feel that their destiny lies in their own hands, that they control their own future. They feel that their future depends upon their own ...

- initiative
- abilities
- plans
- ideas
- energy
- efforts
- works
- discipline
- image
- education
- training
- production

The point is this: because people feel self-sufficient, perfectly capable of handling their own lives. They often put little meaningful trust in God.

As stated before, we not only *should* but *must* plan life and work while on earth. It is the only way to fulfill our purpose for being on earth. But we must seek God's will and guidance, help and care, and acknowledge God as we plan and live out our plans. The great error of a self-sufficient person is acting as if man is the supreme and ultimate end of life—that man can handle his own affairs and life without God. But never forget this: the future of every person on earth is at most a small boat on the stormy and uncertain sea of life.

"Boast not thyself of tomorrow; for thou knowest not what a day may bring forth" (Pr.27:1).

QUESTIONS:
1. What kind of plans do you tend to make without consulting God? In what ways do plans go better when you do include the Lord's counsel?
2. What important truths does an attitude of self-sufficiency ignore?

2. SELF-SUFFICIENCY IS FAILURE TO RECOGNIZE THE UNCERTAINTY OF LIFE (v.14).

There are two reasons why tomorrow is uncertain.

1. Our minds and nature are limited. We simply cannot know the future. No matter what we may plan or think, we do not know what will happen tomorrow; we are completely in the dark. Think for a moment: What will happen tomorrow? We do not know. In fact, we do not know what will happen one hour from now. The point is this: we forget and ignore our nature—who we are, how limited we really are, how uncertain life with all its happenings and events really is. There is a tendency within man to ignore the fact of his frailty and weakness. In all the pride and arrogance of his soul, he wants to be in control of his own life and destiny, to be completely self-sufficient. He wants to have no need whatsoever for God. But this is utter foolishness, for man cannot know what will happen tomorrow. His very nature is limited, so limited that he cannot

know much about what is happening now and very little about what happened in the past. He does not and cannot know about tomorrow.

2. Our lives at most are only as a vapor that appears for a brief time and then vanishes away. Once we are born into this world, the only thing we can know for sure is that we will die; sooner or later we *will all die*.

A vapor appears and can be seen, but it is not solid or substantial or permanent. It is shifted and buffeted about and disappears ever so quickly. We seldom know when death will come or how it will come. But come it will; and when it comes, we are snatched out of this life and cast into eternity, never to return to this life. Therefore, it is utter foolishness to refuse to acknowledge this fact—we simply cannot know the future (or know anything) other than what God reveals to us.

⇒ Living a self-sufficient life apart from God is the depth of foolishness.
⇒ Planning the future without planning for eternity is the depth of foolishness.

> **"For he knoweth our frame; he remembereth that we are dust. As for man, his days are as grass: as a flower of the field, so he flourisheth. For the wind passeth over it, and it is gone; and the place thereof shall know it no more" (Ps.103:14-16).**

ILLUSTRATION:
No individual has any guarantee of another day or even another minute. At any moment our plans may cease for a whole host of reasons.

> *Hank Gathers was a strong, healthy young man and a star on his basketball team at Loyola-Marymount College. In addition, his team was preparing to enter a national basketball tournament. The week before the tournament started, the team was practicing, doing a simple jogging exercise. Hank fell dead right to the gymnasium floor. No one, including Hank, knew anything was wrong—right up to the second he died.*

When will you die? This simple question should pull you back to reality. No one is self-sufficient. We are all utterly dependent upon God.

QUESTIONS:
1. Why is it so tempting to make our plans without God? What are some of the reasons we plan on our own?
2. How does the uncertainty of the future help you to see your need for God?
3. Why is planning apart from God completely foolish? Think about a time when your plans fell to pieces. How could you have handled the situation differently?

3. SELF-SUFFICIENCY IS FAILURE TO ACKNOWLEDGE GOD (v.15).

A person should consult God in his plans and life, but most—by far most—do not. Most people go about living life as they wish; they seldom consider God. But this is not the way life is to be lived. A person is to acknowledge God and confess his dependency upon God. Note that man is said to be dependent upon God for two things.

1. Man is dependent upon God for life. He should say, "If the Lord will, I shall live." This means that whether he lives or not and how he lives is in the hands of God. Therefore, a man should depend upon God for life; he should pray and discuss his life with God, such things as...

- food
- clothing
- housing
- health

- welfare
- protection
- security
- employment

- fulfillment
- joy
- love
- peace

We must trust and depend upon God, fellowship and commune with Him day by day and moment by moment or else He cannot help us. Just think: we can have the love and presence, provision and protection of God; our lives can be in the perfect will of God. We can live and walk upon earth praying and proclaiming to the world: "If He wills, I shall live—my life and future and destiny are in the hands and provision and protection of God, totally and completely in His keeping!"

2. Man is dependent upon God for *all* that he does. He should say, "If the Lord wills, I will do this or that." What this means is that a man is not able to do what he plans unless God wills it—not a single thing. A thousand things can happen to prevent us from carrying out our plans even within the next hour, not to mention tomorrow. Therefore, a person should trust God, pray, and talk over all his ways with God...

- his work
- his relationships
- his schedule
- his activities

No matter what way a person turns, the person should acknowledge God in all his ways. He should be walking and praying all day long, acknowledging God in all his ways: praying for God's will as he does this and that.

"In all thy ways acknowledge him, and he shall direct thy paths" (Pr.3:6).

ILLUSTRATION:

The story is told of a farmer who went to sell a cow. As he passed his neighbor, the farmer told of his big plans. He said, "I am going to sell this cow, put some of the money in the bank, buy a big meal for myself and a present for my wife." His wise neighbor cautioned, "Dear friend, you should say, 'If the Lord wills, you will do these things.'" "Oh, I am going to do them all right. I have my cow right here and off I go," the farmer said.

Later, the farmer came back beaten, bruised and bleeding, with his clothes torn. "What happened?!" the neighbor asked. "I was robbed and they took my cow," the farmer said. "Well, what are you going to do now, go home?" his neighbor asked. "If the Lords wills," the farmer replied.

It is easy to make big plans. We often feel very confident in our own abilities. But one day of bad circumstances can change our feelings completely. It is of the utmost importance that we rely upon God when we make our plans. We must realize and acknowledge that we can do nothing without Him. Therefore, we need His guidance in everything we do.

QUESTIONS:
1. Why are we truly dependent upon God for everything in life? How does this fact affect your life? How should it affect your life?
2. What simple steps should we always take when we plan anything?

4. SELF-SUFFICIENCY IS BOASTING, BRAGGING, AND SHOWING ARROGANCE (v.16).

The word "boastings" means an empty boaster.[37] That is, it is a person who boasts about something he thinks he has, but he does not really have it. He lives in an unreal world. Any person who goes through life without God is like this. He lives and plans, thinking that he controls his life and future. His life is one big boast of self-sufficiency, and it is wrong, totally wrong. A thousand things can happen to change his plans—to injure him or to radically change his life and work, or to snatch his life right out of this world.

Note a fact seldom thought about: most boasting is not done by word of mouth. It is done by the way we live, by flaunting our abilities and successes through our possessions and activities.

We have an urge, a tendency to boast and to be seen and recognized as better or more successful than others. And note what Scripture says: we rejoice in our boastings—that we are more successful in our work than some others. But such boastings—such pride and arrogance—are evil. Why? Because a man's ability and life are due to God and rest in the hands of God.

ILLUSTRATION:
A thought-provoking story is found in Aesop's fables about a fox and a crow.

> One day a fox was walking through the woods when he spied a crow with a piece of cheese in its beak. The fox desperately wanted the cheese, so he began to try to irritate the crow saying, "What an ugly bird you are." The fox thought to himself, "If the crow responds to me with an insult, she will drop the cheese and I will have it for my supper." But the crow was intent on saving the cheese for her young and paid no attention whatever to the fox. Then the fox tried a different approach. He said to the crow, "Oh, but what a beautiful singing voice you have. Of all the birds I have ever heard, truly you are the greatest. If only I could hear one beautiful note." As the fox continued, the crow swelled with pride. Quickly, the crow opened her mouth, let out a squawk, dropping the cheese to the hungry fox below.

Boasting will not only keep us from gaining, it will cost us what we have. Stay humble before God, and He will lift you up.

QUESTIONS:
1. What situations tempt you to speak boastfully? How can you steer away from those situations?
2. How does acknowledging your dependence upon God keep you from prideful boasting?

5. SELF-SUFFICIENCY IS SIN (v.17).

This is a striking definition of sin: to know that we should do something and refuse to do it is sin. As simply stated as possible: when we know to do good and refuse to do it, it is sin. A person is to trust and acknowledge God, to pray and ask God for His presence, guidance, help, care, and strength...
* when he plans today and tomorrow
* when he goes into a city

---

[37] A.T. Robertson. *Word Pictures in the New Testament*, Vol.6, p.56.

- when he continues in the city
- when he buys and sells
- when he gets gain
- when he does this and that

A person is to walk in fellowship and communion with God day by day and moment by moment, acknowledging Him in all his ways. He is to commit his life—all his ways—unto the Lord. Refusing to do so is sin, and the wages of sin is death—spiritual and eternal death.

> **"And every one that heareth these sayings of mine, and doeth them not, shall be likened unto a foolish man, which built his house upon the sand: and the rain descended, and the floods came, and the winds blew, and beat upon that house; and it fell: and great was the fall of it" (Mt.7:26-27).**

QUESTIONS:
1. What happens when we hear the Word of God but do not do it?
2. Why is *not* doing something often a sin? How can you become more aware of the sins of omission?

SUMMARY:

Think for a moment: How often do we casually say, "Tomorrow, I will do this or that," even though we have no promise of even one more breath? Scripture is very direct. We are utterly dependent upon God, completely helpless without Him. For this reason, we must acknowledge that God is our true sufficiency. And for this reason, we must be sure that the Lord is at the center of our planning. We must never forget:
1. Self-sufficiency is planning without God.
2. Self-sufficiency is failure to recognize the uncertainty of life.
3. Self-sufficiency is failure to acknowledge God.
4. Self-sufficiency is boasting, bragging, and showing arrogance.
5. Self-sufficiency is sin.

PERSONAL JOURNAL NOTES:
(Reflection and Response)

1. The most important thing that I learned from this lesson was:

2. The thing that I need to work on the most is:

3. I can apply this lesson to my life by:

4. Closing Prayer of Commitment:

	CHAPTER 5	together for the last days.	for judgment against you
	C. Temptation 3: The Rich Man— Hoarding Wealth, 5:1-6	4 Behold, the hire of the labourers who have reaped down your fields, which is of you kept back by fraud, crieth: and the cries of them which have reaped are entered in the ears of the Lord of sabaoth.	**4. Summons 3: Weep & wail for the way you are living** a. Have cheated, stolen, defrauded
1. A strong summons—weep & wail if you are hoarding wealth	Go to now ye rich men, weep and howl for your miseries that shall come upon you.		
2. Summons 1: Weep & wail, for wealth is not lasting	2 Your riches are corrupted, and your garments are motheaten.	5 Ye have lived in pleasure on the earth, and been wanton; ye have nourished your hearts, as in a day of slaughter.	b. Have lived self-ishly—in pleasure & luxury
3. Summons 2: Weep & wail, for hoarding wealth condemns you	3 Your gold and silver is cankered; and the rust of them shall be a witness		c. Have indulged, fattened yourself for judgment
a. Will be a witness against you	against you, and shall eat your flesh	6 Ye have condemned and killed the just; and he doth	d. Have condemned & killed the righteous
b. Will eat you as fire	as it were fire. Ye	not resist you.	
c. Will be stored up	have heaped treasure		

Section V
TEMPTATIONS AND TRIALS: COMMON TO ALL BUT ESPECIALLY TO THE GIFTED
James 4:11–5:6

STUDY 3: TEMPTATION 3: THE RICH MAN—HOARDING WEALTH

Text: James 5:1-6

Aim: **To reevaluate your living and your giving before the Lord.**

Memory Verse:

> **"Go to now ye rich men, weep and howl for your miseries that shall come upon you" (James 5:1).**

INTRODUCTION:
The rich person faces a fierce temptation, a temptation so powerful that it will consume him unless he lives ever so close to the Lord. What is the temptation that so forcefully attacks the rich? The temptation to bank and hoard money instead of using it to meet the needs of the destitute and dying of the world. The Bible never condemns all rich persons. It only condemns the rich who store up their wealth instead of using it to reach the lost, feed the hungry, cloth the naked, shelter the cold and homeless, nurse the sick, and sound the glorious news of salvation around the world. Within this world that reels under the weight of desperate needs, how can anyone keep more than he needs? How can anyone keep from committing all he is and has to help and minister to people? How can anyone not live and give sacrificially in order to meet the needs of those who are disadvantaged and deprived? God knows that we are without excuse. This is the reason for this passage: to warn all the rich of this world, all who keep more than what they need.

OUTLINE:
1. A strong summons—weep and howl if you are hoarding wealth (v.1).
2. Summons 1: weep and wail, for wealth is not lasting (vv.2-3).
3. Summons 2: weep and wail, for hoarding wealth condemns you (v.3).
4. Summons 3: weep and wail for the way you are living (vv.4-6).

1. A STRONG SUMMONS TO RICH PEOPLE (v.1).

"You rich men, weep and howl for your miseries that shall come upon you" (Js.5:1).

"Weep and howl" here means to burst into weeping and to howl with grief if you are hoarding money.[38] Why? Because *miseries* (plural) are coming upon you—such terrible miseries that you need to begin weeping and wailing now. There will be...
- miseries of afflictions
- miseries of emptiness
- miseries of loneliness
- miseries of insecurity
- miseries of passion
- miseries in judgment
- miseries in hell

Riches that are hoarded will fail a person; they will not satisfy and they will doom a person. They will bring all kinds of miseries upon a person. Therefore, weigh the summons of God.

QUESTIONS:
1. What kind of misery have you seen the love of money cause?
2. How is God summoning you to handle your resources? How does your obedience demonstrate your trust in God rather than in money?

2. GOD'S FIRST SUMMONS—WEEP AND WAIL, FOR WEALTH IS NOT LASTING (vv.2-3).

Note the three things mentioned.
⇒ There are riches that are "corrupted," which means rotted. This would refer to such things as farm produce like wheat or building products like wood. Many a person gains wealth or a lavish living through farming or construction or some other industry whose products eventually rot away.
⇒ There are garments that become moth-eaten. This would include the textile and clothing industries. Many gain their riches or their extravagant lifestyles through these industries.
⇒ There is gold and silver that is cankered or rusted. This refers to mineral, chemical, metal, and mining interests of the economy. James notes that if the minerals lie unused they will no longer shine.

The point is striking, for it is a fact seldom considered. If wealth—money or anything else—is hoarded, it is useless. It does nothing but sit there, and eventually it will be gone. It will never be used for the good that it could do. The rich person who has it will contribute nothing to his generation but...

---

38 A.T. Robertson. *Word Pictures in the New Testament*, Vol.6, p.57.

- produce and buildings that rot
- clothing that is eaten away
- gold and silver that waste away

What a terrible tragedy! To have done nothing for the world but leave the material things that age, rot, decay, and pass away forever and ever. Wealth—riches and material and physical things—does not last.

> **"As the partridge sitteth on eggs, and hatcheth them not; so he that getteth riches, and not by right, shall leave them in the midst of his days, and at his end shall be a fool" (Je.17:11).**

ILLUSTRATION:

> *A minister was visiting his childhood town and wanted to see the little church where he was saved many years before. Arriving at the location, he found that the church had been converted into a home. The owners were very helpful, however, and gave the minister directions to the new building. When he finally arrived at his boyhood church, the minister was shocked to find an enormous beautiful building. But he was saddened to discover from his conversation with the current pastor that the poor were not helped anymore, nor did they feel welcome.*
> *"Well, the church cannot say, 'Silver and gold have I none,'" the new pastor proudly announced to the older minister.*
> *"No," the minister replied, "neither can she say, 'In the name of Jesus Christ of Nazareth, rise up and walk!'"[39]*

Jesus told his disciples, "Freely ye have received, freely give" (Mt.10:8). God does not give to us so that we can hoard for our own comfort. We must generously help others, especially the needy. The most terrible, tragic reality is that the selfish and rich of this world do not even realize their miserable status, nor the horrible judgment that awaits them because of their neglect of the needy.

QUESTIONS:
1. Why is it so foolish to hoard wealth? How can you better focus your thought on eternity to avoid this trap?
2. What is wealth good for? How does a scriptural understanding of wealth affect your outlook on the world? Your church? Your neighbor?

3. GOD'S SECOND SUMMONS—WEEP AND WAIL, FOR HOARDING WEALTH CONDEMNS YOU (v.3).

Wealth will condemn the rich in three ways.
1. Wealth will stand as a witness against the uncaring rich. When? Now and in the day of judgment.
   ⇒ Every person who is concerned with the desperate needs of this world sees that some rich are living selfish lives. They wish that the rich and hoarding would wake up and get to their task of meeting the critical needs of the world.

---

39 Richard A. Steele, Jr. and Evelyn Stone, Editors. *Heartwarming Bible Illustration.* (Chattanooga, TN: AMG Publishers, 1998), #211.

⇒ Every poor and needy person sees that some rich care and that others are heartless or insensitive toward their needs.

⇒ All others in the world, including the rich themselves, see that many rich are hoarding and living selfish lives. But they ignore the fact or do not care enough to change or to fulfill their duty to the world and God.

⇒ Worst of all, God sees those who are living selfish and hoarding lives. Occasionally the rich have to fear the poor, who sometimes rise up against them and threaten to destroy their lives. But the rich must always fear God, for God is the One who can destroy both body and soul in hell.

2. Wealth will consume the whole person as a fire. If we hoard wealth, the passion to increase or stockpile more and more money will burn within us. And the more we hoard, the more we will desire and lust after wealth. Ultimately, the passion for more and more will consume us. We will never be satisfied or fulfilled. The obsession with acquiring more wealth will in time destroy us, both here and now and for all eternity. It will eat our flesh and become the consuming fire and passion of our lives.

> **"But they that will be rich fall into temptation and a snare, and into many foolish and hurtful lusts, which drown men in destruction and perdition. For the love of money is the root of all evil: which while some coveted after, they have erred from the faith, and pierced themselves through with many sorrows" (1 Ti.6:9-10).**

3. Wealth will be stored up as a treasure against us in the last days. This refers to the days of coming judgment when all men will stand and give an account to God. The words *heaping together* picture a person working day by day and hour by hour to heap up treasures on earth and, *at the same time*, heaping up wrath against himself in the terrible day of God's judgment. The wrath heaped up will savagely fall upon the rich person. Why? Because the rich person hoarded while a world of needy people died from hunger, cold, or disease, or were doomed eternally because no one cared enough to share the gospel.

> **"Lay not up for yourselves treasures upon earth, where moth and rust doth corrupt, and where thieves break through and steal: but lay up for yourselves treasures in heaven, where neither moth nor rust doth corrupt, and where thieves do not break through nor steal" (Mt.6:19-20).**

ILLUSTRATION:

The story is often told of a carpenter who had worked many years for the same company. But the carpenter was dishonest. He took shortcuts and had unfortunately learned too well how to do so. The shortcuts enabled the carpenter to pocket a lot of money that should have been spent on the houses. One day, the owner of the company told the carpenter he had a special project for him. The carpenter was told to construct a very special house. As usual, the carpenter used cheaper materials and took many shortcuts. When the project was completed, the owner presented the house to the carpenter as a gift. "I cannot think of a more fitting present for all you have done over the years," the owner of the company told him. Much to his dismay, the carpenter was doomed to live with the penalty of his own shortcomings.—SOURCE UNKNOWN

One day we will all be called to account by God, the Owner of our souls. Live your life in such a way that, when that day comes, you will not be ashamed of what you did with the resources entrusted to you.

QUESTIONS:
1. What do hoarded riches say about a person? Do to a person?
2. How can you avoid the selfishness of hoarding riches?

4. GOD'S THIRD SUMMONS—WEEP AND WAIL FOR THE WAY YOU ARE LIVING (vv.4-6).

Four descriptions are given.
1. Some rich people cheat, steal, and defraud their workers. Note what usually happens when they do: the cheated person cries out to God in his suffering. When he does, God hears him. And note who God is: the Lord of Sabaoth. This is the Hebrew word meaning Lord of hosts or Lord of armies. It refers to God's omnipotence, His unlimited power to help the poor, the disadvantaged, and the oppressed. God will execute judgment, wrath, and hell upon the oppressors. This is exactly what God will do to those who cheat and defraud the workers and laborers of the world. Rich people can steal and defraud...
- by not paying just wages
- by not paying a full hour or day's wage
- by not paying for all the work done
- by withholding more than what they should
- by adding to the bill the laborer owes for supplies
- by adding weight to the scales that measure what is being bought

On and on the list could go as to how the rich cheat the worker and the poor. Scripture has much to say about cheating people out of their due wages.
⇒ The person who lies in order to get wealth is a person seeking death.

> **"The getting of treasures by a lying tongue is a vanity tossed to and fro of them that seek death" (Pr.21:6).**

⇒ The person who oppresses the poor is going to meet a day of severe need.

> **"He that oppresseth the poor to increase his riches, and he that giveth to the rich, shall surely come to want" (Pr.22:16).**

⇒ The person who oppresses the worker will face the judgment of God.

> **"And I will come near to you to judgment; and I will be a swift witness against the sorcerers, and against the adulterers, and against false swearers and against those that oppress the hireling [worker] in his wages, the widow, and the fatherless, and that turn aside the stranger from his right, and fear not me, saith the LORD of hosts" (Mal.3:5).**

Scripture also has much to say about treating workers justly and fairly. No person is to get money by extortion nor to charge more interest or taxes than what he should.

> **"Thou shalt not oppress a hired servant that is poor and needy...at his day thou shalt give him his hire, neither shall the sun go**

down upon it; for he is poor, and setteth his heart upon it: lest he cry against thee unto the LORD, and it be sin unto thee" (De.24:14-15).

2. Rich people who hoard their money live selfishly in the luxury and pleasure of this world. They hoard and build up bank accounts and estates. They seek to live lives of pleasure and gratification, being recognized as successful and powerful people who can have and enjoy what this earth has to offer. Note how selfish living forgets God and the cries of the desperate and needy of the world.

3. People who hoard their money are making themselves fat for the day of slaughter. This is graphic language; nevertheless, it is the warning of God to all of us who bank and hoard more than we need. We are rich in comparison to the poor, needy, and dying of the world. Our hoarding is adding more and more weight for the coming day of slaughter, that is, for the wrath of God's terrible judgment.

4. Some of the rich condemn and kill the righteous, and the righteous do not resist them. Note this: the one person whom the rich dislike the most is the person who teaches self-denial—that we are to give all we are and have to meet the needs of the world. Therefore, the rich reject and condemn the righteous. The rich reject the message of self-denial and sacrificial giving that the righteous practice and teach. In addition, in a society that is given over to covetousness and pleasure, the rich and powerful will even persecute and kill the righteous because of their message.

Note: the righteous do not retaliate. They just keep on proclaiming the glorious message of the gospel of Christ Jesus. They continue to reach out to meet the desperate needs of the starving, diseased, poor, and needy of the world.

"Blessed are ye, when men shall revile you, and persecute you, and shall say all manner of evil against you falsely, for my sake" (Mt.5:11).

QUESTIONS:

1. What will God do if we take advantage of the poor? When will He do these things?
2. What does money tempt you to do? How can you overcome this temptation?
3. Why is the righteous message of giving often rejected? What is the best way you can proclaim this message?

SUMMARY:

Money—just the mention of the word stirs emotions in most people. Tragically, the emotion is often that of clinging and hoarding and acting selfishly. But giving to meet another's need is simple obedience to the royal law of love, to love your neighbor as yourself. We often ignore an opportunity to give because we fear we will not have enough left for ourselves. What foolishness! The Lord has promised to meet all of our needs if we seek first the Kingdom of God.

What does God want you to give? Scripture is clear: you are to give to meet the needs of the deprived, the disadvantaged, the poor—holding nothing back. You must be serious about the summons James gives:

1. A strong summons—weep and wail if you are hoarding wealth.
2. Summons 1: weep and wail, for wealth is not lasting.
3. Summons 2: weep and wail, for hoarding wealth condemns you.
4. Summons 3: weep and wail for the way you are living.

JAMES 5:1-6

PERSONAL JOURNAL NOTES:
(Reflection and Response)

1. The most important thing that I learned from this lesson was:

2. The thing that I need to work on the most is:

3. I can apply this lesson to my life by:

4. Closing Prayer of Commitment:

VI. TEMPTATIONS & TRIALS: COMBATED STEP BY STEP, 5:7-20

A. Step 1: Be Patient—Endure—Keep Your Eyes Focused Upon the Return of the Lord, 5:7-11

1. Be patient, for the Lord is going to come again
2. Be as patient as the farmer, for the Lord's coming is near

a. You must

7 Be patient therefore, brethren, unto the coming of the Lord. Behold, the husbandman waiteth for the precious fruit of the earth, and hath long patience for it, until he receive the early and latter rain.
8 Be ye also patient; stablish your hearts: for the coming of the Lord draweth nigh.
9 Grudge not one against another, brethren, lest ye be condemned: behold the judge standeth before the door.
10 Take, my brethren, the prophets, who have spoken in the name of the Lord, for an example of suffering affliction, and of patience.
11 Behold, we count them happy which endure. Ye have heard of the patience of Job, and have seen the end of the Lord; that the Lord is very pitiful, and of tender mercy.

   strengthen your hearts, focusing upon the Lord's return
  b. You must not grumble—lest you be judged

3. Be as patient as the prophets in suffering, for they believed & spoke in the name of the Lord

4. Be as patient as Job in suffering trials & temptations, for he saw the end of the Lord—that the Lord was full of compassion & mercy

Section VI
TEMPTATIONS AND TRIALS: COMBATED STEP BY STEP
James 5:7-20

STUDY 1: STEP 1: BE PATIENT—ENDURE—KEEP YOUR EYES FOCUSED UPON THE RETURN OF THE LORD

Text: James 5:7-11

Aim: To put trials in perspective by focusing on eternity.

Memory Verse:

> "Be ye also patient; stablish your hearts: for the coming of the Lord draweth nigh" (James 5:8).

INTRODUCTION:

The temptations and trials of life can be terrible and overwhelming at times. If we give in to temptations, they can enslave and destroy us before we know it. Temptations can hook us on the world and its possessions and pleasures or else they can wear down our willpower, devastating families, friendships, finances, even health. The trials of life can unsettle and disrupt our lives, and if we are not on guard, they can crush us through some unforeseen event or accident, disease or death. How can we overcome temptations and trials, conquer and gain sure victory over them? There are two steps. The first step is covered in this passage: *be patient—endure—keep your eyes focused upon the Lord's return.*

OUTLINE:
1. Be patient, for the Lord is going to come again (v.7).
2. Be as patient as the farmer, for the Lord's coming is near (vv.7-9).
3. Be as patient as the prophets in suffering, for they believed and spoke in the name of the Lord (v.10).
4. Be as patient as Job in suffering trials and temptations, for he saw the end of the Lord—that the Lord was full of compassion and mercy (v.11).

1. BE PATIENT, FOR THE LORD IS GOING TO COME AGAIN (v.7).

Time and again Scripture declares in no uncertain terms that Jesus Christ is going to come again and return to earth.

⇒ Christ is coming again to reward every person for his work.

> **"For the Son of man shall come in the glory of his Father with his angels; and then he shall reward every man according to his works" (Mt.16:27).**

⇒ Christ is coming again to separate the sheep from the goats.

> **"When the Son of man shall come in his glory, and all the holy angels with him, then shall he sit upon the throne of his glory: and before him shall be gathered all nations: and he shall separate them one from another, as a shepherd divideth his sheep from the goats" (Mt.25:31-32).**

⇒ Christ is coming again to judge both the living and the dead.

> **"I charge thee therefore before God, and the Lord Jesus Christ, who shall judge the quick [living] and the dead at his appearing and his kingdom" (2 Ti.4:1).**

⇒ Christ is coming again to execute judgment upon the unbelievers or the ungodly of the earth.

> **"And Enoch also, the seventh from Adam, prophesied of these, saying, Behold, the Lord cometh with ten thousands of his saints, to execute judgment upon all, and to convince all that are ungodly among them of all their ungodly deeds which they have ungodly committed, and of all their hard speeches which ungodly sinners have spoken against him [the Lord]" (Jude 14-15).**

⇒ Christ is coming again to judge believers.

> **"For we [believers] must all appear before the judgment seat of Christ; that every one may receive the things done in his body, according to that he hath done, whether it be good or bad" (2 Co.5:10).**

Note also what Scripture declares about the return of Christ and believers. It clearly declares how believers are to live.

⇒ Believers are to occupy themselves, be busy in serving the Lord until He comes.

"And he called his ten servants, and delivered them ten pounds, and said unto them, Occupy till I come" (Lu.19:13).

⇒ Believers are to be without spot and unrebukeable when Christ returns.

"That thou keep this commandment without spot, unrebukeable, until the appearing of our Lord Jesus Christ" (1 Ti.6:14).

⇒ Believers are to deny ungodliness and worldly lusts and live soberly, righteously, and godly until Christ returns.

"Teaching us that, denying ungodliness and worldly lusts, we should live soberly, righteously, and godly, in this present world; looking for that blessed hope, and the glorious appearing of the great God and our Saviour Jesus Christ" (Tit.2:12-13).

⇒ Believers are to live so as not to be ashamed before Christ when He returns.

"And now, little children, abide in him; that, when he shall appear, we may have confidence, and not be ashamed before him at his coming" (1 Jn.2:28).

Now, the whole point of the passage is this: we must be patient—endure all the temptations and trials of life, no matter how strong and terrible their onslaught may be. We must patiently combat their enslaving power and the spirit of discouragement and defeat that can sweep over our souls swiftly and unexpectedly. The Lord is coming, and He is going to reward or judge us. And one thing is sure: none of us want to be condemned when He returns (v.9). Therefore, how can we conquer the temptations and trials of life? How can we overcome them and be sure of being rewarded by the Lord when He returns? There is one way and only one way: be patient—endure—keep your eyes focused on the return of the Lord.

The word "patience" means longsuffering, persevering, enduring. Note: this is a very special kind of patience—a spiritual patience that never gives in; it perseveres and suffers on and on no matter what attacks it. Two significant facts need to be noted about that spiritual patience.

⇒ First, spiritual patience is *not a passive acceptance*. It does not just lay back and accept trials and temptations as though they are a part of life that nothing can be done about. Spiritual patience is an active, fighting endurance that confronts trials and temptations and that sets out to conquer them.

⇒ Second, spiritual patience is a *fruit of the Spirit* (see Ga.5:22-23). When the believer faces some trial or temptation, the Holy Spirit arouses within us the urge to combat the situation and to conquer it. Then it is up to us to respond to the leading of the Spirit, to act on the urge and to persevere. It is up to us to refuse to give in to the enslavement or discouragement or defeat. This kind of patience is spiritual patience—a work of the Holy Spirit—and it can be had only by trusting the Spirit of God. Therefore, the believer must trust the Spirit of God to stir his heart to stand fast against the temptation or trial; then he must exert his own will and energy to conquer the situation. The believer is to stand fast and not give in. He is to struggle and fight, persevere and endure—patiently suffer on and on against the temptation or trial—all the while keeping his eyes fixed on the goal and the end: the return of the Lord Jesus Christ, his wonderful Lord.

ILLUSTRATION:
Perhaps no one illustrates patience better than the farmer. Warren Wiersbe comments:

> If a man is impatient, then he had better not become a farmer. No crop appears overnight (except perhaps a crop of weeds), and no farmer has control over the weather. Too much rain can cause the crop to rot, and too much sun can burn it up. An early frost can kill the crop. How long-suffering the farmer must be with the weather!
>
> He must have patience with the seed and the crop, for it takes time for plants to grow. ... The farmer [has] to wait many weeks for his seed to produce fruit.
>
> Why [does] he willingly wait so long? Because the fruit is "precious" (James 5:7). The harvest is worth waiting for.[40]

"In due season we shall reap, if we faint not" (Ga.6:9).

QUESTIONS:
1. How are we to live, knowing that Christ is coming back? Is your lifestyle a positive testimony to that fact?
2. How can you be more patient in the midst of your trials? Can you help others in their time of need?

2. BE AS PATIENT AS THE FARMER, FOR THE LORD'S COMING IS NEAR (vv.7-9).

The farmer is a good example of the kind of patient waiting believers must have as they wait for the Lord's return. The farmer plants his seed and patiently waits for the early rain to germinate the seed and the later rain to ripen the crop. Note this: the farmer looks forward to the day of harvest with great expectation—so much so that he does all he can to protect the glorious day of harvest. He combats the trials of dry and wet weather, insects and disease, and the wild weeds and briers of the world. No matter what confronts him, the farmer does all he can to conquer the trial. Why does he endure so patiently? Because his eyes are fixed upon the great day of harvest.

The example for believers is strong: "Believers—you also be patient—patiently endure just as the farmer. Do two things."

1. Believers must "establish" their hearts. The word establish means to set upon; to fix upon; to make fast.[41] We must set our hearts upon the Lord's coming, for His coming is near. The idea is that it is drawing ever so close and can happen at any moment. We must focus and set our hearts upon His return—be looking for it every day just as the farmer looks for his great day of harvest. Looking for the great day of redemption—for the Lord's glorious return—will stir us to combat and overcome temptations and trials, no matter how bad the situation may be.

"Therefore, my beloved brethren, be ye stedfast, unmoveable, always abounding in the work of the Lord, forasmuch as ye know that your labour is not in vain in the Lord" (1 Co.15:58).

---

40 Warren W. Wiersbe. *Be Mature.* (Colorado Springs, CO: Chariot Victor Publishing, 1978), p. 154.
41 W.E. Vine. *Expository Dictionary of New Testament Words*, p.41.

2. Believers must not complain about, murmur against, or judge other believers. We must not grumble about our circumstances, our trials and temptations, blaming others for what happens to us. This is one thing God will not tolerate. Note the Scripture: if we complain, murmur, and grumble, we will be condemned. And, "behold, the judge stands before the door." This is a very strong warning.

QUESTIONS:
1. How do your daily actions show faith in God and in His return?
2. Complaining and criticizing keep us from focusing on the Lord's return. How can we keep from doing so when there are so many burdens and trials to bear?

3. BE AS PATIENT AS THE PROPHETS IN SUFFERING AFFLICTION, FOR THEY BELIEVED AND SPOKE IN THE NAME OF THE LORD (v.10).

What James is saying is this: "Look at the prophets. Look at those who have gone before you—men and women who believed and hoped in God and bore witness to God. They faced all kinds of trials and temptations, but they patiently endured, combated, and conquered them all. Look at the prophets, and you will have a great example to follow in patient endurance." They continued to proclaim the salvation and hope of God for the world, continued to believe and to speak up for God. As Hebrews says:

> **"[They suffered] cruel mockings and scourgings, yea, moreoever of bonds and imprisonment: they were stoned, they were sawn asunder, were tempted, were slain with the sword: they wandered about in sheepskins and goatskins; being destitute, afflicted, tormented; (of whom the world was not worthy:) they wandered in deserts, and in mountains, and in dens and caves of the earth" (He.11:36-38).**

ILLUSTRATION:

> *All the children stayed home from school—all except for six-year-old Ruby Bridges.*
> *Every morning, she walked through a heckling crowd to an empty school. White people lined up on both sides of the way and shook their fists at her, simply because she is black. Two U.S. marshals walked ahead of her and two behind her, but she kept coming. Then she spent the day alone with her teachers inside that big silent school building.*
> *In explanation of her courage, Ruby's mother said, "There's a lot of people who talk about doing good, and a lot of people who argue about what's good," but there are other folks who "just put their lives on the line for what's right."*[42]

As believers, we will often be persecuted for doing what the Lord commands. But when it comes to doing right, we must not be swayed by the world's opinions. We must be steadfast, patiently living and proclaiming the salvation of the Lord.

QUESTIONS:
1. Do you think the prophets ever became discouraged?
2. How did the prophets respond despite all of their trials? How can you follow their tremendous example of faithfulness?

---

42 Edward K. Rowell, Editor. *Fresh Illustrations for Preaching and Teaching*, p.34.

4. BE AS PATIENT AS JOB IN SUFFERING TRIALS AND TEMPTATIONS, FOR HE SAW THE END OF THE LORD—THAT THE LORD WAS FULL OF COMPASSION AND MERCY (v.11).

Few people have ever suffered or will ever suffer such trials and temptations of life as Job did. He suffered utter bankruptcy—the loss of all his property, livestock, and employees. And then, in the severest blow of all, he lost all of his sons. In addition to all this, his wife fussed at him because he refused to complain against God for destroying their lives. But note this: Job never gave in to the trials or temptations. He never forsook his faith in God. He did not understand all that was happening to him, but he refused to turn against God. He stood and patiently endured, struggling to conquer all and to do it in the name of the Lord. The point is this: Job kept his eyes fixed upon the Lord and the great hope of the Lord.

> **"Though he slay me, yet will I trust in him" (Jb.13:15).**
> **"The righteous also shall hold on his way, and he that hath clean hands shall be stronger and stronger" (Jb.17:9).**

QUESTIONS:
1. Despite all his trouble, what precious things could never be taken from Job?
2. How did Job keep his faith during the terrible attack of Satan? What are some experiences you have come through that have tried your faith? How did you handle the situations? What might you have done differently?

SUMMARY:

When trials and temptations come, we must focus on Jesus Christ and patiently endure. Be encouraged, for He is all we need. He is our Deliverer. He not only gives us strength in the here and now, but the day is coming when He will return and deliver us from the evils of this world—deliver us eternally!
1. Be patient, for the Lord is going to come again.
2. Be as patient as the farmer, for the Lord's coming draws near.
3. Be as patient as the prophets in suffering, for they believed and spoke in the name of the Lord.
4. Be as patient as Job in suffering trials and temptations, for he saw the end of the Lord—that the Lord was full of compassion and mercy.

PERSONAL JOURNAL NOTES:
(Reflection and Response)

1. The most important thing that I learned from this lesson was:

2. The thing that I need to work on the most is:

3. I can apply this lesson to my life by:

4. Closing Prayer of Commitment:

	B. Step 2: Take Each Circumstance & Respond Properly, 5:12-20		
1. Circumstance 1: When heavily tried, do not curse or swear	12 But above all things, my brethren, swear not, neither by heaven, neither by the earth, neither by any other oath: but let your yea be yea; and your nay, nay; lest ye fall into condemnation.	be forgiven him. 16 Confess your faults one to another, and pray one for another, that ye may be healed. The effectual fervent prayer of a righteous man availeth much.	2) Sins forgiven **4. Circumstance 4: When you have sinned, confess your sins to one another & pray for one another**
2. Circumstance 2: When your experience ranges from affliction to cheerfulness, pray & praise **3. Circumstance 3: When you are sick, call for prayer from church leaders** a. The steps to healing 1) Anoint with oil 2) Pray b. The results 1) Restored, saved	13 Is any among you afflicted? let him pray. Is any merry? let him sing psalms. 14 Is any sick among you? let him call for the elders of the church; and let them pray over him, anointing him with oil in the name of the Lord: 15 And the prayer of faith shall save the sick, and the Lord shall raise him up; and if he have committed sins, they shall	17 Elias was a man subject to like passions as we are, and he prayed earnestly that it might not rain: and it rained not on the earth by the space of three years and six months. 18 And he prayed again, and the heaven gave rain, and the earth brought forth her fruit. 19 Brethren, if any of you do err from the truth, and one convert him; 20 Let him know, that he which converteth the sinner from the error of his way shall save a soul from death, and shall hide a multitude of sins.	a. Because the effective, fervent prayer of a believer works b. Because of the dynamic example of Elijah **5. Circumstance 5: When a believer is backslidden, seek him** a. He is to be sought out & led to repentance b. The results 1) He will be saved from death 2) He will have his sins covered

Section VI
TEMPTATIONS AND TRIALS: COMBATED STEP BY STEP
James 5:7-20

STUDY 2: STEP 2: TAKE EACH CIRCUMSTANCE AND RESPOND PROPERLY

Text: James 5:12-20

Aim: To learn godly responses to trying circumstances.

Memory Verse:

> **"The effectual fervent prayer of a righteous man availeth much"** (James 5:16).

INTRODUCTION:
Life throws at us a great variety of situations. Ultimately, we are not able to control what circumstances we are faced with. How, then, can we be sure to take the right action? To say the right words? How can we combat and conquer the temptations of life?

107

Scripture tells us there are two steps that must be taken in order to live a consistent Christian life. The first step is to be patient and endure, to keep your eyes fixed upon the return of the Lord Jesus Christ. The second step to be taken is the subject of this lesson: to take each circumstance and respond to it appropriately.

OUTLINE:
1. Circumstance 1: when heavily tried, do not curse or swear (v.12).
2. Circumstance 2: when your experience ranges from affliction to cheerfulness, pray and praise (v.13).
3. Circumstance 3: when sick, call for prayer from church leaders (vv.14-15).
4. Circumstance 4: when you have sinned, confess your sins to one another and pray for one another (vv.16-18).
5. Circumstance 5: when a believer is backslidden, seek him (vv.19-20).

1. CIRCUMSTANCE 1: WHEN HEAVILY TRIED OR TEMPTED, DO NOT SWEAR OR CURSE (v.12).

Swearing or cursing is common today, so common that it has tragically become an acceptable practice in society. Note exactly what this verse says: "Above all things, my brothers, swear not at all." Above all things: Scripture puts swearing and cursing right at the top of the list of its prohibitions. Why would Scripture place such a heavy emphasis on not swearing or cursing? Because swearing and cursing are either taking God's name in vain or else showing man's worthlessness. A man's word is a reflection of himself. He is either trustworthy or untrustworthy. If his word is untrue, he has lost his credibility and worth in the eyes of others. It is the truthfulness and reliability of a man's word that is important, that really matters. There should, therefore, be no need for oaths. There should be no need for a man's word to be reinforced. Swearing shows a heart that is disturbed, lacking, or evil. No matter who the person may be—how high or low in society—his words reveal the true condition of his heart: restful, assured, fulfilled, and good or else disturbed, insecure, lacking, and evil.
Note three significant points.
1. There are at least six types of swearing.
   a. There is *swearing by oaths*. Jesus was put under oath to give an answer (Mt.26:63), and Paul swore by taking an oath (2 Co.1:23; Ga.1:20). What then does James mean by saying, "Swear not"? Simply that a man's word should be trustworthy in his day-to-day speech, so trustworthy that no oath is ever necessary. His character should be his guarantee, the only guarantee he needs.
   b. There is *habitual, frivolous swearing*. The unrighteous are said to have "mouths full of cursing and bitterness" (Ro.3:10, 14).
   c. There is *hypocritical swearing*. There are some who "bless God" in one breath and turn around and "curse men" in the next breath. "Out of the same mouth proceedeth blessing and cursing" (Js.3:9-10).
   d. There is *silent, universal swearing*. Every man is charged with secretly cursing others within his heart. "Thine own heart knoweth that thou thyself...hast cursed others" (Ec.7:22).
   e. There is *evasive swearing*. Some do not use words that are foul, dirty, ugly, harsh, or binding. They would never use God's name in vain. Rather, they choose substitute words—words that are commonly used in everyday conversation, words that would never be considered swearing. Others choose what are thought to be milder curse words. By evading harsh swearing, they feel their words are not so improper or sinful. They count themselves less guilty.

f. There is *ego* or *egotistical swearing*. Many swear to boost their ego, their authority, their manliness around others. They feel an identity with the crowd by crossing over to the forbidden.

2. A person is not to swear by heaven or earth nor by any other oath. This is clearly stated by Scripture.

    a. Do not swear by heaven, for it is God's throne: the place where His glory is manifested (Is.66:1). To swear by heaven or to curse heaven is to swear by God and to curse God.

    b. Do not swear by earth, for the earth is God's footstool: the place He governs and looks over (Is.66:1; Ps.24:1). To swear by earth or to curse earth is to swear by God and to curse God.

    c. Do not swear by any other oath, for all power belongs to God. In reality, no man has any power to do anything except what is given by God at that moment. Therefore, he really does not have the power to keep oaths. The recognition of this reality should cause a man to live so honestly and straightforwardly that his word alone is acceptable. Oaths and vows should not be necessary.

Note this: all power belongs to God; therefore, a man should stand in awe of God, not curse Him. But observe what it is that is usually cursed: God and the things of God, the very things that should not be cursed. This says much about the selfish, depraved nature of man. Cursing God is such a terrible sin that it is one of the Ten Commandments. A special judgment is even pronounced upon the curser (Ex.20:7). Cursing is meaningless, thoughtless, and irreverent.

> **"But I say unto you, Swear not at all; neither by heaven; for it is God's throne" (Mt.5:34).**

3. A person is to let his word be so true that it is his guarantee. A man is to need no other words to show his character or strength—no curse words and no swearing words a man should not have to say any more than "yes, I will..." or "no, I will not...." In fact, Jesus Christ said that anything more than straightforward words is rooted in evil. A man's life should be so honest and upright that no one would ever question his word, whether or not something is true, whether or not something will be done or followed through with.

Something that is often overlooked is this fact: swearing and cursing do not make a matter more believable; they really make a matter more suspicious. A person swears something because the issue or his character is questionable. What an indictment of depravity! Yet swearing and cursing are the acceptable habits of men.

> **"But let your communication be, Yea, yea; Nay, nay: for whatsoever is more than these cometh of evil" (Mt.5:37).**

ILLUSTRATION:

Think for a moment about the utter foolishness of profane talk. If what we say is to be thought of as reliable, why would our words need to be "verified" by forceful cursing or flippant swear words? A simple, straightforward statement should be enough to make our point.

A certain senator disliked profanity above all things. This venerable senator had been shocked by the inflammatory interjections of a certain politician, with whom he frequently was compelled to confer. But on all such occasions he would refrain from censuring the culprit except in the mildest manner.

One day when the politician came to the senator's committee room on a subject of considerable importance, the senator indicated a seat to him, and remarked,
"Now, Mr. Blank, before we enter upon a discussion of this question, we shall assume that everybody and everything is damned. Now we can talk it over [in a friendly manner]."[43]

The point is obvious: cursing and swearing do not add to the truthfulness of what we are saying. They only take away from the integrity of our character!

QUESTIONS:
1. People swear or curse for many reasons, but it is always wrong. Why is it not only wrong but foolish to swear or curse?
2. What will really guarantee the truth of our words? How can you strengthen your own testimony?

2. CIRCUMSTANCE 2: WHEN YOUR EXPERIENCES RANGE FROM AFFLICTION TO CHEERFULNESS, PRAY AND PRAISE (v.13).

When we are facing trouble, God wants us first and foremost to seek Him for power and deliverance to walk through the trial or temptation. He wants us to ask Him for courage to be a great witness for Him as we walk through it all. And when we are free of trouble, God wants us praising Him and rejoicing in Him.

1. All kinds of temptations and trials afflict us as believers, in truth, afflict everyone on earth.
   ⇒ There are temptations to drink, do drugs, be immoral, commit adultery, cheat, steal, lie, be prideful, be selfish, and on and on.
   ⇒ There are trials such as accidents, unemployment, ill health, financial difficulties, unfaithfulness of a spouse, any number of disappointments, and on and on.

When such circumstances strike or happen to us, we are to combat them by prayer. We are to pray and seek God for His presence and guidance, His power and strength to walk through the trial. Then we are to ask God for the courage to be a dynamic witness for Him and His glorious salvation.

> **"Watch and pray, that ye enter not into temptation: the spirit indeed is willing, but the flesh is weak" (Mt.26:41).**
> **"And he spake a parable unto them to this end, that men ought always to pray, and not to faint" (Lu.18:1).**

2. Most people on earth also have times when they are free from trials and temptations. As stated, these are times when God wants us walking about praising and worshipping Him. We are to be *cheerful in the Lord*, showing the world that there is joy in the Lord—the joy of assurance and confidence in the eternal salvation and life that Christ provides. This is the praise that is to be constantly flowing from our lips.

> **"Speaking to yourselves in psalms and hymns and spiritual songs, singing and making melody in your heart to the Lord" (Ep.5:19).**

---

[43] Paul Lee Tan. *Encyclopedia of 15,000 Illustrations*, #10099.

QUESTIONS:
1. How have you seen prayer help you through a trial?
2. What good reasons do you have for praising God every day?
3. How is the joy of the Lord in your life evident to others?

3. CIRCUMSTANCE 3: WHEN YOU ARE SICK, CALL FOR PRAYER FROM CHURCH LEADERS (vv.14-15).

1. Note the four facts given in this passage.
   a. "Is any sick among you?" The sick are those who are so sick that they are *shut-ins*—unable to get out to go to the ministers and leaders of the church.
   b. "Is any sick among you? Let him call for the elders [ministers or leaders] of the church." The sick person is to be so concerned over his welfare and so trusting of God that he knows God can heal him. He also believes in prayer, that where two of three are gathered together in the name of Christ, Christ will be there in more power.
   c. "Let them [the elders] pray over him, anointing him with oil **in the name of the Lord**." The elders are to do both of these things *in the name of the Lord*. That is, they are to know and acknowledge that the Lord alone is the Healer of our sicknesses. We are not healed by our prayers nor by oil, but by the Lord. But the elders are also to know two other things:
      ⇒ First, God has commanded us to pray for deliverance and healing in times of affliction and suffering.
      ⇒ Second, God has told us to anoint the sick with oil.

   d. "The prayer of faith shall save the sick, and the Lord shall raise him up...." The Lord will heal the sick person and forgive his sins because of the prayer of faith. This is a difficult passage for many people, because many true believers have prayed in faith for healing—for themselves or for a loved one—and not been healed. Does this mean that Scripture is wrong? Or that God does not carry through with His promises? Not at all! There are several factors to consider when looking at each situation:
      • Is the believer truly praying in faith, believing that God can and will heal?
      • Is the believer praying with the right motive?
      • Is the believer praying for God's will?
      • Is the believer praying for healing so that the Lord will be honored, Him and Him alone?

   Remember: God chooses to heal some and not to heal others. Why? Why would God not heal someone who is suffering and whom He loves? For the same reason God allows us, His children, to go through any other trial or temptation...
      • to test us and prove us
      • to help us learn patience, endurance, and perseverance
      • to use our forbearance and stamina as a testimony to others of God's sustaining grace
      • to bring more glory to God as people see His strengthening, sustaining power at work in us
      • to bring more glory to God through our healing
      • to reach more souls for Christ through our faith and testimony as people see the Lord strengthen us through the suffering

2. Second, picture the scene of what is being said in this passage. A dear, dear brother or sister is so sick that he is bedridden. His sickness is ongoing, unending, so much so that if he is ever going to join us in the worship of the Lord again, the Lord is going to have to miraculously heal him. Our dear brother or sister is hopelessly bedridden and will be so for the rest of his life. What is he or she to do? Just lie there and give in to the trial? Yield to the temptation to limit God's power? What should the elders (ministers and leaders) of the church do? Encourage the dear brother to bear his affliction and suffering—to lie there and accept his affliction with dignity, but with no hope of ever being healed by God?

This passage emphatically says "No!" Neither the dear brother or sister nor the elders should give up to the trial or sickness. As clearly as possible, Scripture says they should do two things:

⇒ Gather around the sick person and pray.
⇒ Gather around the sick person and anoint him with oil.

Now, for a couple of questions.

⇒ Does this work? Is this what God expects us to do when one of our loved ones or dear brothers or sisters become sick? Let us answer these questions by asking several other questions.
⇒ What is there in this passage or in this book that says this is not a clear instruction of Scripture? It would seem that raw honesty before the Lord—without preconceived notions—would require us to say that this instruction stands as the Lord's teaching as much as any other in the book of James.
⇒ Why not do this? What is wrong with going to a dear brother or sister—one whom we love ever so deeply and one who has been *among us* as one of God's faithful worshippers and servants—and putting a little oil on his head and praying for God to heal him? He is a dear brother who is hurting, suffering, and racked with pain, and he has been given no hope. What is wrong with us doing all we can for him? What is wrong with praying with all the faith we can arouse within our hearts and minds?

All believers, of course, have to answer these questions for themselves; but as we answer them, we must be honest—honest to God and His Word and honest to ourselves and our loved ones. There is absolutely no question—these instructions *are* in the Word of God. Their presence and clear teaching cannot be denied. What, then, are we to do? What does God want us to do? Regardless of what men say and do, what does God's Word say?

> **"Verily I say unto you, If ye have faith as a grain of mustard seed, ye shall say unto this mountain, Remove hence to yonder place; and it shall remove; and nothing shall be impossible unto you" (Mt.17:20).**
>
> **"Jesus said unto him, If thou canst believe, all things are possible to him that believeth" (Mk.9:23).**
>
> **"If ye abide in me, and my words abide in you, ye shall ask what ye will, and it shall be done unto you" (Jn.15:7).**

3. Note the instruction to anoint with oil. Why would Scripture tell us to anoint the sick with oil? There are two excellent reasons.

a. Oil is a symbol of the Holy Spirit, of His presence. The oil helps the sick person to focus and concentrate upon the presence of the Holy Spirit and His power. It is often difficult for a sick person to focus. Therefore the oil—its presence and placement upon the body—helps the sick person to concentrate upon the presence and power of the Holy Spirit.

b. Oil is a symbol of God's care, comfort, and joy, of His mercy to us. It is the oil of gladness. Therefore, the presence of the oil is to stir the sick individual to believe in God's will to be merciful and His desire to fill the believer's heart with gladness.

ILLUSTRATION:
Evangelist Charles Price relates this touching story of a deathly sick woman.

> *She said to me "My Brother, do you know what Jesus has done?"*
> *"I know that my Lord doeth all things well," was my reply.*
> *"He has given me His faith," she said. "Honestly, I do not know the moment I received it; but, praise His name, I know it is here."*
> *And it was. That night, the heavenly breezes blew. That night the Christ of the healing road touched, with the power of Omnipotence, the sick, weary body of His needy child. That night a cancer was melted by the touch divine. A mountain was moved by the faith of God which had been imparted to a sick woman by the Lord of Glory Himself.*[44]

What a marvelous story of an ordinary woman in whom God did an extraordinary thing! This woman followed the Scripture, praying for God's mercy, for His healing touch upon her body. And the Lord, with great compassion and mighty power, rewarded her faith right then and there.

QUESTIONS:
1. Have you personally experienced a healing or do you know someone who has? What events or actions preceded the healing?
2. What is your responsibility as a Christian believer when afflicted with severe illness?
3. Why does Scripture tell us to anoint the sick with oil?

4. CIRCUMSTANCE 4: WHEN YOU HAVE SINNED, CONFESS YOUR SINS TO ONE ANOTHER AND PRAY FOR ONE ANOTHER (vv.16-18).

Does this mean that believers are to go around confessing all their sins in all their details and ugliness? No! This is not what this passage is talking about. It is referring to certain types of sins or to certain times when we are to confess our sins. We should confess our sin...
- when the sin has been a wrong or injustice done against someone else
- when we have misled or lied to someone
- when we have offended someone or caused someone to stumble and sin
- when restitution should be made
- when we have publicly committed some crime and public forgiveness is required
- when a trusted minister or Christian counselor may be able to help us in seeking repentance and restoration before God and man

Note why we should confess our sins to one another: so that we, on hearing, can pray for one another. Prayer is of critical importance for many reasons, one of which is stated in verse 16: the effectual, fervent prayer—the earnest, working power of prayer—avails much. Prayer that is truly earnest is a prayer that works and heals a sin-sick soul (v.16).

---

[44] Charles S. Price. *The Real Faith*. (Plainfield, NJ: Logos International, 1940), p.57.

Elijah is an excellent example of the power of prayer. He was a man like us, a human being who had passions and feelings just like we have, who faced the same temptations and trials that we do. Yet Elijah earnestly prayed for it not to rain, and it did not rain for three years and six months. Then he prayed again for it to rain, and it rained and the earth bore its fruit (1 K.17:1f; 18:1f; Lu.4:25). The point is this: prayer—earnest and fervent prayer—is effective; it works. God hears and answers prayer.

> **"Ask, and it shall be given you; seek, and ye shall find; knock, and it shall be opened unto you: for every one that asketh receiveth; and he that seeketh findeth; and to him that knocketh it shall be opened" (Mt.7:7-8).**

QUESTIONS:
1. What are some practical examples of when and why we should confess our faults or sins to one another?
2. Whose prayers does God answer? In what manner do we need to pray for God to move on our behalf? Is this an area where you need to improve?

5. CIRCUMSTANCE 5: WHEN A BELIEVER HAS BACKSLIDDEN, SEEK HIM (vv.19-20).

This is speaking of believers: *brothers, if any of you stray from the truth*. Note that believers can....
- stray away from the truth (v.19)
- walk in the way of error (v.20)

When this happens, the believers of the church are to seek to convert him, that is, to lead him to repentance. The word *convert* means to turn, hence, to take him by the hand and lead him to repentance. What a descriptive picture: loving one another so much that as soon as a believer slips into sin...
- we take him by the hand
- we turn him around and lead him to repent

APPLICATION:
What a different place the church and world would be if we loved one another so much that we actually did this! How desperately such a ministry of restoration is needed today! What is to prevent churches or ministers or teachers from arousing people to set up a ministry of restoration?

Note: if we turn a believer around from his sin, we save his soul from death and cover a multitude of sins. What is meant by death here? The great Greek scholar A.T. Robertson says that the person saved here is a believer being won back to Christ.[45] Once a believer's soul has been saved, restored back to Christ, a multitude of sins becomes covered and forgiven by the blood of Christ. (Please see A CLOSER LOOK below, James 5:19-20, for a full discussion on the subject of the **"Sin Unto Death."**)

> **"Let the wicked forsake his way, and the unrighteous man his thoughts: and let him return unto the LORD, and he will have mercy upon him; and to our God, for he will abundantly pardon" (Is.55:7).**

Note this about temptation and trials: seeking others for the Lord strengthens oneself against temptations and trials. The Christian witness becomes a student of the gospel

---

45 A.T. Robertson. *Word Pictures in the New Testament*, Vol.6, p.67.

and of man. He learns all he can about the faults and needs of men and all he can about God and His provision. The knowledge of both strengthens his own faith.

QUESTIONS:
1. What should we do when a fellow believer strays from the truth?
2. What is the result of converting someone to Christ? Who has the Lord put on your heart to try to lead to Christ?

A CLOSER LOOK # 1
(5:19-20) **Sin—Backsliding—Believer's Judgment**: this passage and that in 1 John 5:16 below both deal with backsliding believers. And both are difficult passages. They are passages where there are almost as many different interpretations as there are words in each passage. The one thing that is clear is this: where James 5:20 is a ray of hope and encouragement to backsliding believers, 1 John 5:16 is a severe warning. It is a warning so severe that one must walk ever so righteously; one must trust the Lord Jesus Christ to grant the power to overcome sin. Because of the correlation between these two difficult passages, we are giving here an in-depth study dealing with the "sin unto death" for those teachers and students of the Bible who wish to delve further into the Scripture.

> **"If any man see his brother sin a sin which is not unto death, he shall ask, and he shall give him life for them that sin not unto death. There is a sin unto death: I do not say that he shall pray for it"** (1 Jn.5:16).

There are several passages of Scripture that issue a severe warning and speak of the sinful behavior of believers...
- sinful behavior that causes loss of all reward by fire—a loss so great one is stripped as much as a burned-out building. It is the loss of all except the bare salvation of oneself (1 Co.3:11-15, esp.v.15).
- sinful behavior that destroys the flesh so that the Spirit may be saved (1 Co.5:5).
- sinful behavior that can cause a person to become a castaway (1 Co.9:27).
- sinful behavior that causes death for a believer (1 Co.11:29-30, esp. v.30; 1 Jn.5:16).
- sinful behavior that merits no escape (He.2:1-3; 12:25f).
- sinful behavior that prohibits a person from ever repenting again (He.6:4f).
- sinful behavior that causes a person to miss God's rest (He.4:1f).
- sinful behavior that prohibits any future sacrifice for sins and merits terrible punishment (He.10:26f).
- sinful behavior that entangles a person in the pollutions of the world after he has come to the knowledge of the Lord Jesus Christ (2 Pe.2:20).
- sinful behavior that leads to death (1 Jn.5:16).

There are basically two positions on the "sin unto death" that need to be looked at and studied.
1. The first position sees the *sin unto death* as being spiritual and eternal death. Some who hold this position believe that it can be committed only by a person who makes a *false profession*; others think that it can be committed by *genuine believers*. Note these facts.

a. First, note the word *brother*. The word *brother* means either true believers or professing believers who commit the *sin unto death*. The person who commits the sin unto death is a *church member*.

b. Second, note that the words life and death must correspond. If it is spiritual and eternal life that God gives to a person, then the sin unto death has to be referring to spiritual and eternal death. (The Greek scholar Marvin Vincent points this out.[46] Note what the verse is saying:

"[God] shall give him life for them that sin not unto death" (v.16).

What kind of life is John talking about? Physical or spiritual life? The context points strongly to spiritual and eternal life. This has been the whole discussion of this passage: for example...

"He that hath the Son hath life; and he that hath not the Son of God hath not life" (v.12).

Again, if the life that God gives is spiritual and eternal life, then the sin unto death must correspond; it must mean the opposite, that is, spiritual and eternal death. Note what the full verse says:

"If any man see his brother sin a sin which is not unto death, he shall ask, and he shall give him [spiritual] life for them that sin not unto death. There is a sin unto death [spiritual death]: I do not say that he shall pray for it" (v.16).

c. Third, does this mean that a believer can commit sin to the point that he is doomed to spiritual and eternal death? If so, what do we do with passages of Scripture where God assures Christ that He will never lose a single brother who genuinely believes in Him? Passages and promises such as these...

- God will allow no genuine believer to be plucked out of His hand.

  "And I give unto them eternal life; and they shall never perish, neither shall any man [no one, Greek (includes Satan)] pluck them out of my hand. My Father, which gave them me, is greater than all; and no man is able to pluck them out of my Father's hand" (Jn.10:28-29).

- God has predestinated believers to the image of Christ so that Christ will have many brothers.

  "For whom he did foreknow, he also did predestinate to be conformed to the image of his Son, that he might be the firstborn among many brethren" (Ro.8:29).

- God will perform the work of salvation and growth until the day of Jesus Christ.

---

[46] Marvin Vincent. *Word Studies In The New Testament*, Vol.1. (Grand Rapids, MI: Eerdmans Publishing Co., 1969), p.371.

"Being confident of this very thing, that he which hath begun a good work in you will perform it until the day of Jesus Christ" (Ph.1:6).

- God keeps the believer by His power.

"Who are kept by the power of God through faith unto salvation ready to be revealed in the last time" (1 Pe.1:5).
"I know whom I have believed, and am persuaded that he is able to keep that which I have committed unto him against that day" (2 Ti.1:12).
"Now unto him that is able to keep you from falling, and to present you faultless before the presence of his glory with exceeding joy, to the only wise God our Saviour, be glory and majesty, dominion and power, both now and ever" (Jude 24-25).

To repeat the question above, does the sin unto death mean that a believer can commit sin to the point that he is doomed to spiritual and eternal death?

⇒ Once a person is *born again* by the Spirit of God, can he be *unborn*?
⇒ Once a person receives the divine nature of God, once the divine nature has been incorporated into the fiber of his being, can the divine nature be taken away and unincorporated? (See 2 Pe.1:4.)
⇒ Once a person has been given the incorruptible seed and nature, can he again become corruptible? (See 1 Pe.1:23; 1 Pe.1:3-4.)
⇒ Once a person has been created into *a new creature* in Christ, can he become the *old creature* again? (See 2 Co.5:17.)
⇒ Once a person is transformed from the *old man* into the *new man*, can he be re-transformed and changed back into the *old man*? (See Ep.4:22-24.)
⇒ Once the Spirit of God enters a person's life and turns the person's body into a *holy temple*, does the Spirit ever leave a person? (See Jn.14:16-17; 1 Co.3:16-17; 6:19-20.)
⇒ Once our Lord Jesus Christ Himself has entered the life of a person, does God ever lose the life to such a point that His Son has to leave the life? (See Jn.14:16-18; 14:20; 17:23; Ga.2:20; Col.1:27; Re.3:20.)

Now note: all this would have to be possible and would have to happen if the sin unto death refers to a genuine believer. Does the sin unto death refer...
- to a genuine believer or to a professing believer?
- to a person who looks like a brother but is a false believer?

John himself refers to some professing believers who had committed the terrible sin of denying Christ. He calls them antichrists (plural), persons who had been in the church and who had professed Christ, but who had turned away from Christ and stood opposed to Him.

Note that these persons had been in the church, but they had forsaken Christ and had left the church. Picture the scene: there would still be friends and perhaps family members in the church who loved them and cared for them and who wanted them to be led back to Christ and His church. Therefore, they would be praying for them to return. But note: their sin is so great that John does not encourage people to pray for them. He does not forbid it, but he does not encourage it. He simply says: "I do not say that he [the true believer, the loved one] shall pray for it [the sin unto death]."

Note what John says about these whom he calls antichrists:

> **"Little children, it is the last time: and as ye have heard that antichrist shall come, even now are there many antichrists; whereby we know that it is the last time.** *They went out from us, but they were not of us***; for if they had been of us, they would no doubt have continued with us: but they went out, that they might be made manifest that they were not all of us"** **(1 Jn.2:18-19).**

d. Now what is the sin unto death? Greek scholar Marvin Vincent says that it is "the tendency...to cut the bond of fellowship with Christ....[it is] whatever breaks the fellowship with the soul and Christ, and, by consequence, with the individual and the body of believers...for there is no life apart from Christ." He says that the sin arises from the character of a person who is "alien from God." That is, the person never knew God, not really. His profession was false to begin with.[47] Kenneth Wuest, also a Greek scholar, says,

> *"The sin unto death" refers in the context in which John is writing, to the denial of the Incarnation...it would be committed by those whom John designates as antichrists, who did not belong to the true Christian body of believers, but were unsaved.*[48]

Kenneth Wuest also quotes the Greek scholar Henry Alford of the Alford Greek Testament as saying:

> *There are those who have gone out from us, not being of us (2:19), who are called antichrists, who not only "have not" Christ, but are Christ's enemies, denying the Father and the Son (2:22), whom we are not even to receive into our houses nor to greet (II John 10, 11). These seem to be the persons pointed out here, and this is the sin, namely, the denial that Jesus is the Christ, the incarnate Son of God. This alone of all sins bears upon it the stamp of severance from Him who is the Life itself. As the confession of Christ, with the mouth and in the heart, is salvation unto life (Rom.10:9), so denial of Christ with the mouth and in the heart, is sin unto death."*[49]

A.T. Robertson, another Greek scholar, says:

> *John conceives of a sin that is deadly enough to be called "unto death"....There is a distinction in Heb.10:26 between sinning wilfully after full* knowledge *and sins of ignorance (Heb.5:2). Jesus spoke of the unpardonable sin (Mk.3:29; Mt.12:32; Lk.12:10), which was attributing to the devil the manifest work of the Holy Spirit. It is possible that John has this idea in mind when he applies it to those who reject Jesus Christ as God's Son and set themselves up as antichrists.*[50]

William Barclay says that the Greek for "sin unto death" (harmatia pros thanaton) means "the sin which is going towards death, the sin whose end is death, the sin which, if continued in, must finish in death."[51] He says that the sin is...

---

[47] Marvin Vincent. *Word Studies in the New Testament*, Vol.1, p.371.

[48] Kenneth Wuest. *In These Last Days.* "Word Studies in the Greek New Testament," Vol.4. (Grand Rapids, MI: Eerdmans Publishing Co., 1946), p.181.

[49] Ibid., p.181.

[50] A.T. Robertson. *Word Pictures in the New Testament*, Vol.6, p.243f.

[51] William Barclay. *The Letters of John and Jude.* (Philadelphia, PA: Westminster Press, 1958), p.142.

- persistent sin
- obstinate sin
- deliberate sin
- cold-blooded sin
- wide open sin
- purposeful sin

He says that the *sin unto death* is committed by a man…
- who persists in sin
- who rejoices in sin
- who never thinks of temptation as a sin
- who has no regret for sinning
- who glories in his sin
- who boasts in his sin
- who is proud of his sin
- who is proud that he knows how to get away with his sin
- who delights in sin

In his usual descriptive way, William Barclay describes the person who commits the *sin unto death*:

> Now in life it is a fact of experience that there are two kinds of sinners….So long as a man in his heart of hearts hates sin and hates himself for sinning, so long as he knows that he is sinning, he is never beyond repentance, and, therefore, never beyond forgiveness; but once a man begins to revel in sin, and to make sin the deliberate policy of his life, and loses all sense of the terror and the awfulness of sin, and also the feeling of self-disgust, he is on the way to death, for he is on the way to a state where the idea of repentance will not, and cannot enter his head.
>
> The sin unto death is the state of the man who has listened to sin so often, and refused to listen to God so often, that he has come to a state when he *loves his sin, and when he regards sin as the most profitable thing in the world.*[52]

The conclusion of this interpretation would be one of two:

First, there are some who conclude that the sin unto death refers to a professing believer, a person who makes a profession only, a false profession. Therefore, he was never really converted…
- never born again
- never indwelt by the Holy Spirit
- never filled with the divine nature
- never indwelt by Christ
- never made into a new man
- never created into a new creature
- never filled with the incorruptible nature

Because of this, the person is easily led back into the world and into sin. He leaves the fellowship of believers and of the church and returns to the possessions and pleasures of the world. He stands opposed to Christ, not really believing that Jesus Christ is the Son of God.

---

52   William Barclay. *The Letters of John and Jude*, p.142.

Second, there are others who conclude that the sin unto death refers to genuine believers. The person who commits the sin unto death was genuinely converted, but he now becomes unconverted.

⇒ He loses his *new birth*; he is no longer born again.

⇒ He loses his *divine nature*; it is taken from him.

⇒ He loses the *Holy Spirit*; the Holy Spirit leaves the body of the believer and turns the body back into a temple for sin and death.

⇒ He loses the *new man*; his new man is re-transformed back into the old man.

⇒ He loses the creation of the *new creature*; he is recreated back into the old creature.

⇒ He loses the indwelling presence of Christ; God loses the sinner to the point that Christ has to leave him.

Now note: as stated in the beginning, if the life that God gives is spiritual and eternal life, then the sin unto death has to be spiritual and eternal death. Therefore, the person who commits the sin is either a genuine believer or only a professing believer, a person making a false profession. John does call the person a *brother*. Therefore, we can say that this means he is definitely a genuine believer. Or, we can say that every professing believer in the church *looks* like a brother to us, but many are not. They are making a false profession, and very practically, we cannot always tell who is a genuine brother and who is a false brother. We can say that John knew this as well as we do; therefore, he is calling every church member a brother, but making it clear that some are making a false profession. They are committing *sin that leads to death*. Whatever position we take, we must make sure that we are taking it because we are convinced that it is the teaching of God's Word. We must never hold a position because of such things as denomination, church, friends, teachers, or education. We must study the Word and let the Word interpret and speak for itself. And where there are difficult passages, we must come to the best conclusion we can under the guidance of the Holy Spirit. There is no question that the warnings of Scripture given to believers are some of the most difficult passages to interpret in all of Scripture. Perhaps God has deliberately made them this way to warn us how terrible sin is, that we must watch and guard against sin—that sin points to a false profession—that sin can and does lead to severe consequences—that we must be careful to make our profession sure and steadfast—that we can not deliberately and wilfully sin and be obstinate and hardened in sin, not without suffering the most severe consequences.

2. The second position sees the sin unto death as referring to physical death. Briefly stated, these commentators say that the person is a genuine believer who falls into sin so deeply that he has to be severely disciplined by God and taken on home to be with Him. They look at the passage dealing with the sinful behavior of believers and say that a believer can continue in sin and can practice sin, and that there is no question about this. The believer still has freedom of choice.

And despite the tug and the pull of the Holy Spirit within, every honest believer knows what it is to succumb and give in to sin. Most believers even know what it is to practice sin for awhile without repentance. It is only the longsuffering of God that convicts and that leads to repentance.

This position would say this: perhaps it is possible for a believer to continue in sin so long that he reaches a point of no return (see note—Ac.5:5-6). He is so rooted and imbedded in sin that God knows he will never repent. Now if such is possible, only God could know it. Only God can know the heart of a man to such a point that He knows the future of the man. If a man reaches that point of no repentance, his testimony and service on earth is forever ruined and forever useless. In fact, he has brought disrepute and dishonor to the name of Christ. He has harmed the Lord's cause, and so long as he is on earth, he will continue to add to the sin of the world and to heap abuse upon the name of Christ. His very purpose for living upon the earth as a Christian is lost and gone forever. The desire to return to the Lord and to live for Him, and to witness to His saving grace will never be aroused in his heart again. God knows this. But despite all this, God still loves him. And God has determined, for Christ's sake, that His purpose will be fulfilled in every single believer (Ro.8:29). Not a single believer shall be plucked out of His hand (Jn.10:28). Thus, God takes the believer on to be with Him. God goes ahead and unites the believer with Christ, His dear Son (see 1 Co.11:29-30).

There are several examples in Scripture that seem to be warning and speaking to men about the same sinful behavior. There is the example...

- of Moses' death (De.32:48-52).
- of Israel and the golden calf (Ge.32:1-35).
- of the man who gathered sticks on the Sabbath right after the Sabbath was instituted (Nu.15:32-36).
- of Nadab and Abihu (Le.10:1-2).
- of Korah (Nu.16:31-34).
- of Achan (Jos.7:16-26).
- of Uzziah (2 S.6:1-7).
- of Ananias and Sapphira (Ac.5:1-11).
- of the man who had slipped into a shameful immoral sin (1 Co.5:1-5).
- of some who had slipped into sin and were mocking God by partaking of the Lord's Supper without repenting (1 Co.11:27-30).

Oliver Greene says:

> What IS "the sin unto death"? The best place to find the answer is in Paul's letter to the church at Corinth. If you will study the eleventh chapter of 1 Corinthians in its entirety, you will find that some of the believers were grievously misbehaving at the Lord's table, making gluttons of themselves and drinking until they became intoxicated.... "FOR THIS CAUSE many are weak and sickly among you, AND MANY SLEEP (are dead)."
>
> **Paul also warned the Corinthian Christians that if they would judge themselves, repent of their misbehaving in the house of God and straighten up, God would not be forced to judge them; but if they did not judge themselves, God would have no alternative but to judge and chasten them, that they should "not be condemned with the world" (1 Co.11:32).**
>
> The "sin unto death" therefore is continually rebelling against light. When a believer knows what he should do, when he is convicted that he should do it, and yet he refuses to obey the Holy Spirit and the Word of God, he is in danger of committing the sin unto death.
>
> We have another instance of this in 1 Corinthians 5:1-5, when immorality was found in the church. A young man had taken his father's wife and was guilty of fornication. There are those who will not agree that this young man was saved and had committed the sin unto death, but Paul clearly told the other believers in the church what action they should take in the matter:
>
> "In the name of our Lord Jesus Christ, when ye are gathered together, and my spirit, with the power of Lord Jesus Christ, to deliver such an one unto satan, for the destruction of the flesh, that the spirit may be saved in the day of the lord Jesus" (1 Cor.5:4, 5).
>
> Beloved, it is clear that the sin unto death has nothing to do with the salvation of the soul; it has to do with the destruction of the body. Such a person will "suffer loss, but he himself shall be saved; yet so as by fire" (1 Cor.3:12-15). All reward is lost, and such a one will stand before God

empty handed. What that will mean, I confess I do not know; but according to the passage from 1 Corinthians, the person who loses his reward will "suffer loss" - not loss of soul and spirit, but loss of eternal reward.[53]

Oliver Greene gives an excellent illustration in the life of Abraham:

> But *"there IS a sin unto death," and when a believer has committed that sin there is no point in praying for him. In the life of Abraham we find an illustration of a time when it was useless to pray. In Genesis 18:20-30 God revealed to Abraham that He was going to destroy Sodom and Gomorrah. Abraham knew that his nephew Lot and his family were living in Sodom, so he drew near to God and asked, "Wilt thou also destroy the righteous with the wicked? Peradventure there be fifty righteous within the city: wilt thou also destroy and not spare the place for the fifty righteous that are therein?" The Lord replied, "If I find in Sodom fifty righteous within the city, then I will spare all the place for their sakes." But there could not be fifty righteous men found in all of Sodom - and Abraham continued to pray until the number was reduced to ten - just ten righteous people in the great city of Sodom. And the Lord said, I will not destroy it for ten's sake." But God knew that ten righteous ones could not be found in the city, and verse 33 tells us that "THE LORD WENT HIS WAY, as soon as He had left communing with Abraham."*
>
> *With God there is a stopping place, a limit; and Abraham had reached that limit in his intercession for Sodom. God ceased communing with him and left him. What God actually said in departing was, "Abraham, there is no need to pray any longer. There is no need for you to make further request. Pray no more for Sodom, for that city must be destroyed!" When a city or an individual has committed such sin, there is no reason for any Christian to pray for that city or that individual.*
>
> *There are times when we should no longer pray for certain people, there are times when we should no longer witness to certain people. Concerning things spiritual Jesus said, "Give not that which is holy unto the dogs, neither cast ye your pearls before swine, lest they trample them under their feet, and turn again and rend you" (Matt.7:6).*[54]

Thought 1. Whatever our position, we must always remember this: the answer to sin is repentance and confession. As long as a person is still alive, he can repent and confess his sin and God will forgive him and restore him into the fellowship of His dear Son. As long as we are living, there is still hope; there is assurance of forgiveness and cleansing if we will only repent and confess.

> **"I tell you, Nay: but, except ye repent, ye shall all likewise perish" (Lu.13:3).**
> **"Repent ye therefore, and be converted, that your sins may be blotted out, when the times of refreshing shall come from the presence of the Lord" (Ac.3:19).**
> **"Repent therefore of this thy wickedness, and pray God, if perhaps the thought of thine heart may be forgiven thee" (Ac.8:22).**
> **"In whom we have redemption through his blood, the forgiveness of sins, according to the riches of his grace" (Ep.1:7).**
> **"If we confess our sins, he is faithful and just to forgive us our sins, and to cleanse us from all unrighteousness" (1 Jn.1:9).**

53 Oliver Greene. *The Epistles of John.* (Greenville, SC: The Gospel Hour, Inc., 1966), p.211.
54 Ibid., p.210.

> **"Let the wicked forsake his way, and the unrighteous man his thoughts: and let him return unto the LORD, and he will have mercy upon him; and to our God, for he will abundantly pardon"** (Is.55:7).

SUMMARY:

The circumstances of life are anything but predictable. God made the world that way for a reason—He expects us to live by faith. As true believers, we are to do more than just mentally believe in God. We are to have real faith, a faith that is evident in our actions:

1. When we are heavily tried, we will not curse or swear.
2. When our experience ranges from affliction to cheerfulness, we will pray and praise.
3. When we are sick, we will call for prayer from church leaders.
4. When we have sinned, we will confess our faults to one another and pray for one another.
5. When one is backslidden, we will seek him.

PERSONAL JOURNAL NOTES:
(Reflection and Response)

1. The most important thing that I learned from this lesson was:

2. The thing that I need to work on the most is:

3. I can apply this lesson to my life by:

4. Closing Prayer of Commitment:

OUTLINE & SUBJECT INDEX

JAMES

JAMES

REMEMBER: When you look up a subject and then turn to the Scripture reference, you have not only the Scripture but also *an outline and a discussion* (commentary) of the Scripture and subject.

This is one of the *GREAT VALUES* of *THE TEACHER'S OUTLINE & STUDY BIBLE*™. Once you have all the volumes, you will have not only what all other Bible indexes give you, that is, a list of all the subjects and their Scripture references, *BUT* you will also have...

- an outline of *every* Scripture and subject in the Bible
- a discussion (commentary) on every Scripture and subject
- every subject supported by other Scriptures or cross-references

DISCOVER THE GREAT VALUE for yourself. Quickly glance below to the very first subject of the Index of *Second Timothy*. It is:

ABRAHAM
Faith of. Proved his faith by works. 2:21-24

Turn to the reference. Glance at the Scripture and the outline of the Scripture, then read the commentary. You will immediately see the GREAT VALUE of the INDEX of *THE TEACHER'S OUTLINE & STUDY BIBLE*™.

OUTLINE AND SUBJECT INDEX

ABRAHAM
Faith of. Proved his faith by works. 2:21-24

ADULTERY - ADULTERESS
Kinds of **a**. Spiritual **a**. Apostasy toward God. 4:4
Spiritual **a**.. (See **ADULTERY, SPIRITUAL**)

ADULTERY, SPIRITUAL
Discussed. 4:4
Is worldliness. 4:4
Meaning. 4:4
Verses. List of. 4:4

ARROGANCE
Illustrated. Two men of **a**. 2:18

BACKBITING
Discussed. 4:11-12

BACKSLIDING
Duty. To seek the **b**. believer. 5:19-20

BOASTS - BOASTING
Caused by. Tongue. 3:5
Discussed. 4:16
Fact. Is sin. 4:16

COMMITMENT
Meaning. 3:17-18

COMPLETE
Meaning. 1:1-3

CONFESS - CONFESSION
Duty. To **c**. faults to one another. 5:16-18

CONVERSION
Meaning.
A turning from error. 5:19-20
A turning from one's own way. 5:19-20
Results.
Sins covered. 5:19-20
Soul saved. 5:19-20

CRITICISM
Discussed. 4:11-12
Fact. Is sin common to the gifted. 4:11-12
Results. Condemns one. 5:9

CROWN OF LIFE
Meaning. 1:12

CURSING
Discussed. 5:12

DEATH
Caused by. Sin. Backslidden
believer. 5:19-20

DESIRE
Meaning. 1:14-16

DEVIL (See **SATAN**)

DEVOTION
Duty. To draw near God. 4:8

DISCRIMINATION
Discussed. 2:1-13

DISTRUST
Results.
Prayerlessness. 4:3
Temptations and trials. 4:3

DIVISION - DISSENSION
(See **CRITICISM; JUDG-
ING; UNITY**)
Described as. Earthly, sen-
sual, devilish. 3:14-16

DOUBLE-MINDEDNESS
Duty. Not to be **d**. 1:5-8
Fact.
Is unstable. 1:6-8
Shows a need to purify
the heart. 4:8

DOUBT - DOUBTING
Duty. Not to be **d**. 1:5-8

ENDURE - ENDURANCE
Duty.
To **e**., combating tempta-
tion & trials. 5:7-11
To **e**., keeping one's eyes
fixed upon the return of
Christ. 5:7-11
Outline of. 1:3-8

ENTICE - ENTICEMENT
Meaning. 1:14-16; 4:1; 4:2

FAITH
Discussed. Dead vs. living **f**.
2:14-26
Duty. Not to waver in **f**.
1:5-8
Stages - Kinds.
Dead **f**. 2:14-26
True vs. false **f**. 2:14-26
Wavering. 1:5-8
Vs. works. Discussed. 2:14-26

FARMER
Illustrates.
Patience needed to com-
bat temptation & trials.
5:7-9
Patience of **f**. Needed by
believer in waiting for
the Lord's return. 5:7-9

FAVORITISM
Discussed. 2:1-13
Temptation of. Discussed.
2:1-13

FLESH (See **CARNAL**)
Meaning. The struggle
within fighting against
what one should do. 4:2;
4:4

FORGIVENESS, SPIRITUAL
How one receives. Through
prayer. 5:14-15

GENTLE - GENTLENESS
Meaning. 3:17-18

GIFTS, SPIRITUAL
Described. Teaching. Is a
great gift. 3:1

GOD
Goodness of. Discussed.
1:17-18

GOSSIP
Discussed. 4:11-12

HEAL - HEALING
Duty. To pray for healing
when seriously sick. 5:14-15

HIGH IN LIFE, THE (See
RICH, THE)
Discussed. 1:9-11

HUMANISM
Discussed. Is five things.
4:13-17

HUMILITY
Duty. Must humble our-
selves. 4:10
Results.
Exaltation. 4:10
God pours out His grace
upon the humble. 4:6

HYPOCRISY, WITHOUT
Meaning. 3:17-18

**JAMES, THE BROTHER OF
JESUS**
Discussed. 1:1

JESUS CHRIST
Deity. Is God, that is, Elo-
him and Yahweh. 1:1
Fact. Is drawing near. 5:8-9
Return. Duty. To keep one's
eyes fixed upon Jesus in
combating temptation &
trials. 5:7-11

JEWS
Of the diaspora. 1:1

JOB
Example of.
Patience needed to com-
bat temptation & trials.
5:11
Patience needed to wait
for the Lord's return.
5:11

JOY
Essential. To combat temptation. 1:2-4
Source. How to have **J**. in
trials. 1:2-4

JUDGE - JUDGING OTHERS
Discussed. 4:11-12
Sin of. Usurps God's right
to **j**. Makes one as God.
4:12

JUDGMENT
Caused by. Showing partial-
ity. 2:12-13
Fact.
Common to the gifted.
4:11-12
To be reciprocal. 2:12-13
Surety of. To be reciprocal.
2:12-13

KNOWLEDGE
Meaning. 1:5-8; 3:13

LAW
Fact. Breaking one **l**. makes
one guilty of breaking all **l**.
2:8-11

128

LIBERTY (See **LICENSE;**
SANCTIFICATION;
SEPARATION)
Described. Perfect law of
liberty. 1:25
Duty. l. keeps the law. 1:25
Results. l. keeps the law.
1:25

LIFE
Fact. Uncertain. 5:7
Status in. Discussed. 1:9-11

LONGSUFFERING
Meaning. 5:7

LOT
Duty. To rejoice in one's l.
in life. 1:9-11; 4:13; 4:14-16
Status in life. Discussed.
1:9-11

LOWLY IN LIFE, THE
Discussed. 1:9-11

LUST
Discussed. 4:1; 4:1-3; 4:2
Meaning. 1:14-16

MAN
Duty. To rejoice in whatever
state. 1:9-11

MATURITY
Fact. Is revealed by the
tongue. 3:1-12

MERCY
Meaning. 3:17-18

MINISTER - MINISTERS
Duty. To anoint & pray for
the sick. 5:14-15

PARTIALITY
Discussed. 2:1-13
Temptation to show P. Dis-
cussed. 2:1-13

PARTIALITY, WITHOUT
Meaning. 3:17-18

PATIENCE
Duty.
To be **p**. in combating all
temptation & trials.
5:7-11

To be **p**., keeping your
eyes fixed upon the re-
turn of Christ. 5:7-11
Example of.
Patience needed to com-
bat temptation & trials.
5:10
Patience needed to wait
for the Lord's return.
5:10
Meaning. 1:3-4

PEACEABLE
Meaning. 3:17-18

PERFECT
Meaning. 1:3-4

PLAN - PLANNING
Without God. 4:13-17

PLEASURE
Discussed. 4:1; 4:1-3; 4:2

PRAISE
Duty. To **p**. to conquer afflictions. 5:13

PRAY - PRAYER
Duty.
To **p**. to be healed when
seriously sick. 5:14-15
To **p**. to conquer afflic-
tions. 5:13
Fact. Is the source for re-
ceiving all things. 4:2
How.
Fervently. 5:16-18
Persevering - continuing.
5:16-18
Lack of. (See
PRAYERLESSNESS)
Results - Assurance. Is the
answer to *having*. 4:2
When. When one is sick.
5:14-15

PRAYERLESSNESS
Cause. Temptation & trials.
4:3

PRIDE
Results.
God's resistance. 4:5-6
Boasting. 3:3-5

PROFESSION, FALSE
Discussed. 2:14-26

PURE
Meaning. 3:17-18

RAHAB
Faith of. Proved her faith by
works. 2:25-26

REASONABLE - REASON-
ABLENESS
Meaning. 3:17-18

RELIGION
True **r**.
Discussed. 1:27
Is to visit the needy & to
separate from the world.
1:27
Is to visit the orphans &
widows. 1:27

RELIGIONISTS (See **FALSE**
TEACHERS; PHARISEES;
PROFESSION ONLY;
RELIGION)
Discussed. 2:14-26

RESIST
Meaning. 4:7

REWARDS
Described. As crown of life.
1:12

RICH - RICHES
Discussed. 5:1-6
Sin of. Hoarding & banking.
5:1-6
Warning against. Discussed.
5:1-6

RICH, THE
Discussed. 1:9-11

SALVATION - SAVED
Deliverance - Purpose.
Saves a soul & hides a
multitude of sins. 5:19-20
How one is **s**. By a faith that
works & lives. 2:14-26
Results. Saves & hides a
multitude of sins. 5:19-20

SATAN
Duty. To resist. 4:7
How to combat - overcome.
Resist; do not give place
to. 4:7

SELF-DEPENDENCE
Discussed. 4:13-17

SELF-SUFFICIENCY
Discussed. Is five things. 4:13-17

SICK - SICKNESS
Duty. To pray when seriously s. 5:14-15

SIN
Acts - Behavior of.
Boasting. 4:16
Cursing - swearing. 5:12
Double-mindedness. 1:6-8
Grumbling - complaining. 5:9
Hoarding wealth. 5:1-6
Humanism. 4:13-17
Lust. 1:14-16; 4:1-6
Not understanding true wisdom. 3:13-18
Partiality - favoritism. 2:1-13
Profession only. 2:14-26
S. unto death. 5:20
Self-confidence. 4:13-17
Selfishness. 4:1-6
The tongue. 3:1-12
Common to believers.
Professing faith without works. 2:14-16
Showing partiality & favoritism. 2:1-13
Common to teachers. 3:1-18
Misunderstanding true wisdom. 3:13-18
Misusing the tongue. 3:1-12
Common to the gifted. 4:11-5:16
Boasting self-confidence. 4:13-17
Hoarding wealth. 5:1-6
Judging others. 4:11-12
Deliverance. Is hid through conversion. 5:19-20
Fact. Not of the nature of God. 1:13-18
Results. The S. unto death. 5:19-20
Source of. Discussed. 1:14-16

SPEAKING EVIL
Discussed. 4:11-12
Meaning. 4:11-12

SPIRITUAL ADULTERY (See **ADULTERY, SPIRITUAL**)

STATUS
Of life. Duty. To be content with. 1:9-11

STRIFE
Meaning. 3:14-16

SUBMIT
Meaning. 4:7

SUFFERING
Deliverance through. Prayer saves the sick. 5:14-15
Purpose. To teach prayer. 5:14-15

SWEARING
Discussed. 5:12
Wrong of. 5:12

TEACHERS
Duty. To teach if called. 3:1
Temptations of.
Temptations common to teachers. 3:1-18
Misusing the tongue. 3:1-12
Work of. Speech is the major tool. 3:1

TEACHING
Duty. To live a consistent life--what one teaches. 3:13-18; 3:14-16
False.
Discussed. 3:14-16
Vs. true. Discussed. 3:13-18

TEMPTATION
Basic facts. Discussed. 1:2-27
Cause of. Four C. 4:1-6
Discussed. 1:2; 4:1-6
Duty.
To endure until Jesus returns. 5:7-11
To prepare to conquer. Three preparations. 1:19-27
Essential. An attitude of joy. 1:2-4
How to overcome.
Combat step by step. 5:7-20

Discussed. 1:5-12; 4:7-10
Four ways. 4:7-10
Must know two things. 4:5-6
Kinds of.
Boasting self-confidence. 4:13-17
Common to all believers. 2:1-26
Common to teachers. 3:1-18
Common to the gifted. 4:11-5:6
Hoarding wealth. 5:1-6
Judging others. 4:11-12
Misunderstanding true wisdom. 3:13-18
Misusing the tongue. 3:1-12
Professing faith without works. 2:14-26
Showing partiality & favoritism. 2:1-13
Origin.
Discussed. 1:13-15; 1:13-18; 4:1-3; 4:5
Lust, envy, pride. 4:1-3; 4:5
Not of the nature of God. 1:13-18
Purpose. To test & prove us. 1:2
Results.
Death. 1:14-16
Twofold. 1:3-4
What T. does. 1:2-4
Rewards for conquering. Discussed. 1:12
Work of. Stirs endurance. 1:2

TONGUE
Described as.
A world of iniquity. 3:6
Fire. 3:6
Speaking evil. Discussed. 4:11-12
Unruly evil. 3:8
Discussed. 1:19-27; 3:1-12
Speaking vs. listening. 1:19-27
Duty. To bridle. 1:26
Sins of.
Misusing the T. 3:1-12
Swearing. 5:12
Tamed only by Christ. 3:8

TRANSGRESSION
Of law. Breaking one law makes one guilty of all laws. 2:8-11

TRIALS
Basic facts. Discussed. 1:2-27
Discussed. 1:2
Essential. An attitude of joy. 1:2-4
How to conquer. Discussed. 1:12
Purpose. To test & prove us. 1:2
Results. Twofold. 1:3-4
Rewards for conquering. Discussed. 1:12
Work of. Stirs endurance. 1:2

WAR
Discussed. 4:1-3

WAVER - WAVERING
Duty. Not to W. 1:5-8

WEALTH
Fact. A rich man can know God. 1:9-10

View of. Christian's perspective of. 1:7-11

WISDOM
False.
Discussed. 3:13-18
Source of. 3:14-16
Vs. true w. 3:13-18
Meaning. 1:5-8; 3:13-18; 3:13
Source. Discussed. 1:5-8
True.
Discussed. 3:13-18
Vs. false w. 3:13-18

WITNESS - WITNESSING
Results.
Hides a multitude of sins. 5:19-20
Saves a soul. 5:19-20

WORD OF GOD
Duty.
To be a doer & not a hearer only of the Word. 1:22-25
To hear the Word. 1:19-21

WORKS
Vs. faith. Discussed. 2:14-26

WORKS, GOOD
Meaning. 3:17-18

WORLD
Duty. To be unspotted by the w. 1:27

WORLDLINESS
Deliverance from. How to conquer. 4:4-5
Described. As adulteresses & adulterers. 4:4
Discussed. 4:4
Results.
Causes temptations & trials. 4:4
Makes one an enemy of God. 4:4

ILLUSTRATION INDEX

JAMES

ILLUSTRATION INDEX

SUBJECT	SCRIPTURE REFERENCE	PAGE NUMBER
ALLUREMENT (See **TEMPTATION**)		
AVARICE (See **GREED; SERVICE; WEALTH**)		
BACKBITING (See **GOSSIP; SIN**)		
BELIEF (See **FAITH**)		
BELIEVERS (See **FAITH; JUDGMENT; TEMPTATION; TRIALS; WISDOM**)		
BIBLE (See **WORD OF GOD**)		
BLESSINGS (See **HUMILITY**)		
BOASTING (See **HUMILITY**) • The unforeseen cost of pride	Js.4:16	92
CHARACTER (See **WISDOM**)		
CHRISTIANITY (See **FAITH**)		
CIRCUMSTANCES (See **BOASTING; PATIENCE; TRIALS**)		
CONDEMNATION (See **JUDGMENT; PREJUDICE**)		
CONQUERING (See **TEMPTATION; TRIALS**)		
CONSCIENCE (See **RELIGION**)		
CRITICISM (See **JUDGMENT; PREJUDICE**)		
CROWN OF LIFE (See **HEAVEN**)		
CURSING • A distraction from the truth	Js.5:12	109
DANGER (See **TEMPTATION**)		
DEATH (See **SELF-SUFFICIENCY**)		
DECEPTION (See **TEMPTATION**)		
DELIVERANCE (See **TEMPTATION**)		
DESIRE (See **PRAYER – PRAYING**)		
DESTRUCTION (See **TEMPTATION**)		
DIRECTION (See **WISDOM**)		
ENDURANCE (See **HEAVEN; PATIENCE; SUFFERING**)		
EQUITY (See **PREJUDICE**)		
EVANGELISM (See **FAITH; PREJUDICE; WITNESSING**)		

ILLUSTRATION INDEX

SUBJECT	SCRIPTURE REFERENCE	PAGE NUMBER
EVIL (See **GOSSIP; SIN; TEMPTATION**)		
FAITH (See **HEALING; TRIALS; TRUST; WITNESSING**)		
• Faith that touches others	Js.2:15–17	44
• Faith that makes a difference	Js. 2:19–20	46
• Proof of your profession	Js.2:25–26	48
• Faith that overcomes	Js.1:5–8	18
FAITHFULNESS (See **GOSSIP**)		
FAVORITISM (See **PREJUDICE**)		
FOOLISHNESS (See **WISDOM**)		
FUTURE (See **SELF-SUFFICIENCY**)		
GODLINESS (See **GOSSIP**)		
GOSSIP (See **SIN**)		
• Drawing the line between evil and good	Js.4:11	83
• You cannot take it back	Js.3:5–6	53
GREED (See **SERVICE; WEALTH**)		
• Payday is coming!	Js.5:3	97
HEALING		
• Faith that triumphs over trials	Js.5:14–15	112
HEAVEN (See **PATIENCE**)		
• Keep your eyes on the prize	Js.1:12	20
HELP (See **HUMILITY**)		
HOARDING (See **GREED; SERVICE; WEALTH**)		
HUMILITY (See **BOASTING**)		
• The key to God's mercy	Js.4:5–6	73
JOY (See **TRIALS; TEMPTATION**)		
JUDGMENT		
• Reaping what you sow	Js.2:12–13	40
• Give mercy—get mercy	Js.4:11	85
KNOWLEDGE (See **WISDOM**)		
LIFE (See **SELF-SUFFICIENCY**)		
LONGSUFFERING (See **HEAVEN; PATIENCE**)		
LYING (See **TRUTH**)		
MARTYR (See **WISDOM**)		

ILLUSTRATION INDEX

SUBJECT	SCRIPTURE REFERENCE	PAGE NUMBER
MATURITY (See **WISDOM**)		
MEEKNESS (See **WISDOM**)		
MERCY (See **JUDGMENT**)		
MIRACLES (See **HEALING**)		
MONEY (See **WEALTH**)		
MORTALITY (See **SELF-SUFFICIENCY**)		
MOTIVE (See **PRAYER – PRAYING**)		
NEEDS (See **TRUST**)		
OBEDIENCE (See **WISDOM; WORD OF GOD**)		
• Obedience is better than sacrifice	Js.1:22-25	31
OVERCOMING (See **TEMPTATION; TRIALS**)		
PARTIALITY (See **PREJUDICE**)		
PATIENCE (See **HEAVEN**)		
• Heaven: worth it's "wait" in gold	Js.5:7	104
PERSEVERANCE (See **TEMPTATION; TRIALS**)		
PERSISTENCE (See **TEMPTATION; TRIALS**)		
PIETY (See **GOSSIP**)		
PLANNING (See **SELF-SUFFICIENCY**)		
PRAYER – PRAYING		
• Giving God our wants	Js.4:3	70
PREFERENCE (See **PREJUDICE**)		
PREJUDICE (See **WITNESSING**)		
• The gospel knows no boundaries	Js.2:4–7	38
• Real love is unconditional	Js.2:1	36
PREPARATION (See **TEMPTATION; TRIALS**)		
PRIDE (See **BOASTING; HUMILITY**)		
PRIZE (See **HEAVEN**)		
PROFESSION (See **FAITH; PREJUDICE; WITNESSING**)		
PROVISION (See **PRAYER – PRAYING; TRUST**)		

ILLUSTRATION INDEX

SUBJECT	SCRIPTURE REFERENCE	PAGE NUMBER
PURITY (See **RELIGION**)		
RELIABILITY (See **TRUTH**)		
RELIGION		
• Following the Word not the world	Js.1:27	33
RESPONSIBILITY (See **TEMPTATION**)		
REWARD (See **HEAVEN; PATIENCE**)		
RICHES (See **WEALTH**)		
SCRIPTURE (See **WORD OF GOD**)		
SELF-SUFFICIENCY		
• Your ticket to failure	Js.4:14	90
• Plowing ahead without God	Js.4:15	91
SERVICE (See **WEALTH; WITNESSING**)		
• Staying busy for God	Js.1:1	6
SIN (See **GOSSIP; TEMPTATION**)		
• Is your tongue out of control?	Js.3:2	51
SOWING AND REAPING (See **BOASTING; JUDGMENT**)		
STEADFASTNESS (See **GOSSIP; HEAVEN; PATIENCE; SUFFERING**)		
STEWARDSHIP (See **GREED; SERVICE; WEALTH**)		
STRENGTH (See **TRIALS**)		
SUFFERING (See **WITNESSING**)		
• Paying the price for truth	Js.5:10	105
SWEARING (See **TRUTH**)		
TEACHERS (See **GOSSIP; JUDGMENT; SIN; WISDOM**)		
TEMPTATION (See **TRIALS**)		
• Make the difficult choices	Js.4:8	79
• Placing blame where it is due	Js.1:13	24
• It is, oh, so inviting	Js.1:14–16	25
• The lure of the forbidden	Js.4:7	78
TESTING (See **TEMPTATION; TRIALS**)		
TONGUE (See **GOSSIP; SIN**)		

ILLUSTRATION INDEX

SUBJECT	SCRIPTURE REFERENCE	PAGE NUMBER
TRIALS (See **TEMPTATION**)		
• Growing stronger through trials	Js.1:2	11
• Perseverance pays dividends	Js.1:2	12
TRUST		
• Asking for and accepting God's provision	Js.4:2	69
UNCERTAINTY (See **SELF-SUFFICIENCY**)		
WANTS (See **PRAYER – PRAYING**)		
WEALTH (See **GREED; SERVICE**)		
• Money only goes so far	Js.1:9–11	19
• The downfall of many a man and ministry	Js.5:2-3	96
WISDOM	Js.1:4	14
• God's passport to security		
WITNESSING (See **FAITH; PREJUDICE; SUFFERING**)		
• Use it or lose it!	Js.1:1	6
WORD OF GOD (See **FAITH**)		
• Pay attention! There will be a test.	Js.1:19–21	30
WORDS (See **TRUTH**)		
WORKS (See **FAITH; SERVICE; WITNESSING**)		
WORLDLINESS (See **WEALTH**)		
WRONGDOING (See **BOASTING; GREED; SIN; TEMPTATION**)		

ACKNOWLEDGMENTS AND BIBLIOGRAPHY

Every child of God is precious to the Lord and deeply loved. And every child as a servant of the Lord touches the lives of those who come in contact with him or his ministry. The writing ministries of the following servants have touched this work, and we are grateful that God brought their writings our way. We hereby acknowledge their ministry to us, being fully aware that there are so many others down through the years whose writings have touched our lives and who deserve mention, but the weaknesses of our minds have caused them to fade from memory. May our wonderful Lord continue to bless the ministry of these dear servants, and the ministries of us all as we diligently labor to reach the world for Christ and to meet the desperate needs of those who suffer so much.

THE GREEK SOURCES

1. *Expositor's Greek Testament*, Edited by W. Robertson Nicoll. Grand Rapids, MI: Eerdmans Publishing Co., 1970.

2. Robertson, A.T. *Word Pictures in the New Testament*. Nashville, TN: Broadman Press, 1930.

3. Thayer, Joseph Henry. *Greek-English Lexicon of the New Testament*. New York: American Book Co.

4. Vincent, Marvin R. *Word Studies in the New Testament*. Grand Rapids, MI: Eerdmans Publishing Co., 1969.

5. Vine, W.E. *Expository Dictionary of New Testament Words*. Old Tappan, NJ: Fleming H. Revell Co.

6. Wuest, Kenneth S. *Word Studies in the Greek New Testament*. Grand Rapids, MI: Eerdmans Publishing Co., 1953.

THE REFERENCE WORKS

7. *Cruden's Complete Concordance of the Old & New Testament*. Philadelphia, PA: The John C. Winston Co., 1930.

8. Josephus' *Complete Works*. Grand Rapids, MI: Kregel Publications, 1981.

9. Lockyer, Herbert, Series of Books, including his Books on *All the Men, Women, Miracles, and Parables of the Bible*. Grand Rapids, MI: Zondervan Publishing House.

10. *Nave's Topical Bible*. Nashville, TN: The Southwestern Co.

11. *The Amplified New Testament*. (Scripture Quotations are from the Amplified New Testament, Copyright 1954, 1958, 1987 by the Lockman Foundation. Used by permission.)

12. *The Four Translation New Testament* (Including King James, New American Standard, Williams - New Testament In the Language of the People, Beck - New Testament In the Language of Today.) Minneapolis, MN: World Wide Publications.

ACKNOWLEDGMENTS AND BIBLIOGRAPHY

13. *The New Compact Bible Dictionary*, Edited by T. Alton Bryant. Grand Rapids, MI: Zondervan Publishing House, 1967.

14. *The New Thompson Chain Reference Bible.* Indianapolis, IN: B.B. Kirkbride Bible Co., 1964.

THE COMMENTARIES

15. Barclay, William. *The Letters of James and Peter*. Philadelphia, PA: Westminster Press, 1958.

16. Bruce, F.F. *The Epistle to the Colossians*. Westwood, NJ: Fleming H. Revell Co., 1968.

17. _____. *Epistle to the Hebrews*. Grand Rapids, MI: Eerdmanns Publishing Co., 1964.

18. _____. *The Epistles of John*. Old Tappan, NJ: Fleming H. Revell Co., 1970.

19. Criswell, W.A. *Expository Sermons on Revelation*. Grand Rapids, MI: Zondervan Publishing House, 1962-66.

20. Greene Oliver. *The Epistles of John*. Greenville, SC: The Gospel Hour, Inc., 1966.

21. _____. *The Epistles of Paul the Apostle to the Hebrews*. Greenville, SC: The Gospel Hour, Inc., 1965.

22. _____. *The Epistles of Paul the Apostle to Timothy & Titus*. Greenville, SC: The Gospel Hour, Inc., 1964.

23. _____. *The Revelation Verse by Verse Study*. Greenville, SC: The Gospel Hour, Inc., 1963.

24. Henry, Matthew. *Commentary on the Whole Bible*. Old Tappan, NJ: Fleming H. Revell Co.

25. Hodge, Charles. *Exposition on Romans & on Corinthians*. Grand Rapids, MI: Eerdmans Publishing Co., 1972-1973.

26. Ladd, George Eldon. *A Commentary On the Revelation of John*. Grand Rapids, MI: Eerdmans Publishing Co., 1972-1973.

27. Leupold, H.C. *Exposition of Daniel*. Grand Rapids, MI: Baker Book House, 1969.

28. Newell, William R. *Hebrews, Verse by Verse*. Chicago, IL: Moody Press.

29. Robertson, A.T. *Studies in the Epistle of James*. Nashville, TN: Broadman Press.

30. Strauss, Lehman. *Devotional Studies in Philippians*. Neptune, NJ: Loizeaux Brothers.

31. _____. *Colossians & 1 Timothy*. Neptune, NJ: Loizeaux Brothers.

32. _____. *The Book of the Revelation*. Neptune, NJ: Loizeaux Brothers.

33. *The New Testament & Wycliffe Bible Commentary*, Edited by Charles F. Pfeiffer & Everett F. Harrison. New York: The Iverson Associates, 1971. Produced for Moody Monthly. Chicago Moody Press, 1962.

34. *The Pulpit Commentary*, Edited by H.D.M. Spence & Joseph S. Exell. Grand Rapids, MI: Eerdmans Publishing Co., 1950.

35. Tasker, RVG. *The General Epistle of James*. "Tyndale New Testament Commentaries." Grand Rapids, MI: Eerdmans Publishing Co., 1956.

36. Thomas, W.H. Griffith. *Hebrews, A Devotional Commentary*. Grand Rapids, MI: Eerdmans Publishing Co., 1970.

37. _____. Griffith. *Studies in Colossians & Philemon*. Grand Rapids, MI: Baker Book House, 1973.

38. *Tyndale New Testament Commentaries*. Grand Rapids, MI: Eerdmans Publishing Co., Began in 1958.

39. Walker, Thomas. *Acts of the Apostles*. Chicago, IL: Moody Press, 1965.

40. Walvoord, John. *The Thessalonian Epistles*. Grand Rapids, MI: Zondervan Publishing House, 1973.

OTHER SOURCES

41. Berry, John, Editor. *Foxe's Book of Martyrs*. Grand Rapids, MI: Baker Books, 1978.

42. Colson, Charles. *The Difference Faith Makes*, on BreakPoint, December 19, 2002.

43. *God's Little Devotional Book*. Tulsa, OK: Honor Books, Inc., 1995.

44. Green, Michael P. *1500 Illustrations for Biblical Preaching*. Grand Rapids, MI: Baker Books, 2000.

45. Jones, G. Curtis. *1000 Illustrations for Preaching and Teaching*. Nashville, TN: Broadman Press, 1986.

46. Knight, Walter B. *Knight's Master Book of 4,000 Illustrations*. Grand Rapids, MI: Eerdmans Publishing Co., 1994.

47. Krivolahvek, Ken. *Rejoicin' an' Repentin'*. Olathe, KS: KLK Ministries, 2002.

48. Kyle, Ted and John Todd. *A Treasury of Bible Illustrations*. Chattanooga, TN: AMG Publishers, 1995.

49. Macartney, Clarence E. *Macartney's Illustrations*. New York, NY: Abingdon Press, 1946.

50. McHenry, Raymond. *McHenry's Stories for the Soul*. Peabody, MA: Hendrickson Publishers, 2001.

51. Price, Charles S. *The Real Faith*. Plainfield, NJ: Logos International, 1940.

52. Reed, John W. *1100 Illustrations from the Writings of D. L. Moody*. Grand Rapids, MI: Baker Books, 1990.

53. Rowell, Edward K., Editor. *Fresh Illustrations for Preaching and Teaching*. Grand Rapids, MI: Co-published by Christianity Today, Inc., and Baker Books, 1997.

54. Smith, James. *Handfuls on Purpose*, 10 vols. Grand Rapids, MI: Eerdmans Publishing Co., 1947.

55. Steele, Jr., Richard A. and Evelyn Stoner, Editors. *Heartwarming Bible Illustration*. Chattanooga, TN: AMG Publishers, 1998.

56. _____. *Practical Bible Illustrations from Yesterday and Today*. Chattanooga, TN: AMG Publishers, 1996.

57. Tan, Paul Lee. *Encyclopedia of 15,000 Illustrations*. Rockville, MD: Assurance Publishers, 1988.

58. Wiersbe, Warren W. *Be Mature*. Colorado Springs, CO: Chariot Victor Publishing, 1978.

OUTLINE BIBLE RESOURCES

This material, like similar works, has come from imperfect man and is thus susceptible to human error. We are nevertheless grateful to God for both calling us and empowering us through His Holy Spirit to undertake this task. Because of His goodness and grace, *The Preacher's Outline & Sermon Bible*® New Testament is complete, and Old Testament volumes are releasing periodically.

The Minister's Personal Handbook and other helpful **Outline Bible Resources** are available in printed form as well as releasing electronically on WORDsearch software.

God has given the strength and stamina to bring us this far. Our confidence is that as we keep our eyes on Him and grounded in the undeniable truths of the Word, we will continue working through the Old Testament volumes. The future includes other helpful Outline Bible Resources for God's dear servants to use in their Bible Study and discipleship.

We offer this material first to Him in whose Name we labor and serve and for whose glory it has been produced and, second, to everyone everywhere who preaches and teaches the Word.

Our daily prayer is that each volume will lead thousands, millions, yes even billions, into a better understanding of the Holy Scriptures and a fuller knowledge of Jesus Christ the Incarnate Word, of whom the Scriptures so faithfully testify.

You will be pleased to know that Leadership Ministries Worldwide partners with Christian organizations, printers, and mission groups around the world to make Outline Bible Resources available and affordable in many countries and foreign languages. It is our goal that *every* leader around the world, both clergy and lay, will be able to understand God's Holy Word and present God's message with more clarity, authority, and understanding—all beyond his or her own power.

LEADERSHIP MINISTRIES WORLDWIDE
PO Box 21310 • Chattanooga, TN 37424-0310
423) 855-2181 • FAX (423) 855-8616
info@outlinebible.org
www.outlinebible.org - FREE Download materials

LEADERSHIP MINISTRIES WORLDWIDE ▧OBR

Publishers of Outline Bible Resources

Currently Available Materials, with New Volumes Releasing Regularly

- **THE PREACHER'S OUTLINE & SERMON BIBLE® (POSB)**

NEW TESTAMENT

Matthew I (chapters 1-15)	1 & 2 Corinthians
Matthew II (chapters 16-28)	Galatians, Ephesians, Philippians, Colossians
Mark	1 & 2 Thess., 1 & 2 Timothy, Titus, Philemon
Luke	Hebrews, James
John	1 & 2 Peter, 1, 2, & 3 John, Jude
Acts	Revelation
Romans	Master Outline & Subject Index

OLD TESTAMENT

Genesis I (chapters 1-11)	1 Kings	Jeremiah 1 (chapters 1-29)
Genesis II (chapters 12-50)	2 Kings	Jeremiah 2 (chapters 30-52),
Exodus I (chapters 1-18)	1 Chronicles	Lamentations
Exodus II (chapters 19-40)	2 Chronicles	Ezekiel
Leviticus	Ezra, Nehemiah, Esther	Daniel/Hosea
Numbers	Job	Joel, Amos, Obadiah, Jonah,
Deuteronomy	Proverbs	Micah, Nahum
Joshua	Ecclesiastes, Song of Solomon	Habakkuk, Zephaniah, Haggai,
Judges, Ruth	Isaiah 1 (chapters 1-35)	Zechariah, Malachi
1 Samuel	Isaiah 2 (chapters 36-66)	*New volumes release periodically*
2 Samuel		

KJV Available in Deluxe 3-Ring Binders or Softbound Edition • NIV Available in Softbound Only

- **The Preacher's Outline & Sermon Bible New Testament — 3 Vol. Hardcover • KJV – NIV**

- *What the Bible Says to the Believer* — **The Believer's Personal Handbook**
  11 Chs. – Over 500 Subjects, 300 Promises, & 400 Verses Expounded - Italian Imitation Leather or Paperback

- *What the Bible Says to the Minister* — **The Minister's Personal Handbook**
  12 Chs. - 127 Subjects - 400 Verses Expounded - Italian Imitation Leather or Paperback

- **Practical Word Studies In the New Testament** — 2 Vol. Hardcover Set

- **The Teacher's Outline & Study Bible™ - Various New Testament Books**
  Complete 30 - 45 minute lessons – with illustrations and discussion questions

- **Practical Illustrations — Companion to the POSB**
  Arranged by topic and Scripture reference

- **What the Bible Says Series – Various Subjects**
  Prayer • The Passion • The Ten Commandments • The Tabernacle

- **Software – Various products powered by WORDsearch**
  New Testament • Pentateuch • History • Prophets • Practical Word Studies • Various Poetry/Wisdom

- **Topical Sermons Series – Available online only**
  7 sermons per series • Sermons are from the Preacher's Outline & Sermon Bible

- **Non-English Translations of various books**
  Included languages are: Russian – Spanish – Korean – Hindi – Chinese – Bulgarian – Romanian –
  Malayalam – Nepali - Italian – Arabic
  • Future: French, Portuguese

— Contact LMW for Specific Language Availability and Prices —

For quantity orders and information, please contact:
LEADERSHIP MINISTRIES WORLDWIDE or Your Local Christian Bookstore
PO Box 21310   • Chattanooga, TN 37424-0310
(423) 855-2181 (9am – 5pm Eastern) • FAX (423) 855-8616
E-mail - info@outlinebible.org Order online at www.outlinebible.org

PURPOSE STATEMENT

LEADERSHIP MINISTRIES WORLDWIDE

exists to equip ministers, teachers, and laymen in their understanding, preaching and teaching of God's Word by publishing and distributing worldwide *The Preacher's Outline & Sermon Bible®* and related **Outline Bible Resources**, to reach & disciple men, women, boys and girls for Jesus Christ.

MISSION STATEMENT

1. To make the Bible so understandable – its truth so clear and plain – that men and women everywhere, whether teacher or student, preacher or hearer, can grasp its message and receive Jesus Christ as Savior, and…

2. To place the Bible in the hands of all who will preach and teach God's Holy Word, verse by verse, precept by precept, regardless of the individual's ability to purchase it.

Outline Bible Resources have been given to LMW for printing and especially distribution worldwide at/below cost, by those who remain anonymous. One fact, however, is as true today as it was in the time of Christ:

THE GOSPEL IS FREE, BUT THE COST OF TAKING IT IS NOT

LMW depends on the generous gifts of believers with a heart for Him and a love for the lost. They help pay for the printing, translating, and distributing of **Outline Bible Resources** into the hands of God's servants worldwide, who will present the Gospel message with clarity, authority, and understanding beyond their own.

LMW was incorporated in the state of Tennessee in July 1992 and received IRS 501 (c)(3) nonprofit status in March 1994. LMW is an international, nondenominational mission organization. All proceeds from USA sales, along with donations from donor partners, go directly to underwrite our translation and distribution projects of **Outline Bible Resources** to preachers, church and lay leaders, and Bible students around the world.